The Multiple Staff and the Larger Church

The Multiple Staff and the Larger Church

Lyle E. Schaller

ABINGDON

NASHVILLE

THE MULTIPLE STAFF AND THE LARGER CHURCH

Copyright © 1980 by Abingdon

Library of Congress Cataloging in Publication Data

SCHALLER, LYLE E.
   The multiple staff and the larger church.
   Includes bibliographical references.
   1. Big churches. 2. Church officers. 3. Clergy—Office. I. Title.
BV637.9.S32   253   79-20796

ISBN 0-687-27297-1

Portions of this book are based on material which first appeared in the following
periodicals. Grateful acknowledgement is made to *The Lutheran* for, "How To Know
When Your Church Needs More Staff" (February 1, 1978), copyright 1978 by *The
Lutheran;* and *The Clergy Journal* for, "Barriers To Developing Team Ministries" (March
1978), copyright 1978 by Church Management, Inc.

MANUFACTURED BY THE PARTHENON PRESS AT
NASHVILLE, TENNESSEE, UNITED STATES OF AMERICA

To
Herald B. Monroe
C. Philip Alexander

Contents

Preface

Approximately one-half of all Protestant congregations in the United States and Canada average fewer than 75 at worship on a typical Sunday morning, and three-fourths of all churches report fewer than 300 confirmed members. If the worshiping congregation is used as the basic frame of reference in looking at Protestant Christianity on the North American continent, the small church dominates the scene. In some denominational families the dominant expression of the worshiping congregation is the small church with a part-time minister. In the United Methodist Church, for example, less than one-third of all congregations have a full-time resident pastor who has no other employment, is not in school, and does not serve any other congregation. Several expert observers predict that by 1987 one-half of all Southern Baptist preachers will be "dual role" or "bi-vocational" ministers who combine a secular job with pastoring a church. One reason for this prediction is that in 1979 approximately three out of ten Southern Baptist pastors combined preaching with secular employment.

If, however, the focus is changed from counting churches to looking at the place of worship for church members, a radically different picture emerges. In broad general terms one-half of all Protestant church members on the continent can be found in one-sixth of the churches and one-fourth of them can be found in approximately 6 percent of all congregations.

This large concentration of church members in a relatively small proportion of congregations is represented in the following denominational statistics: 7 percent of all Southern Baptist Convention churches with 1000 or more members account for 32 percent of all Southern Baptists. Six and a half percent of all American Lutheran Church parishes with more than 1000 confirmed members include 26.5 percent of the confirmed members of that denomination. Slightly less than one-third of all United Presbyterians are members of congregations with more than 1000 communicants, yet these large congregations account for only 8 percent of all United Presbyterian churches in the nation. One-third of all Episcopal parishes account for approximately three-quarters of all Episcopal communicants. The 2500 United Methodist congregations with more than 800 members represent less than 7 percent of all churches in that denomination, but account for 31 percent of the membership. Only 5 percent of all parishes in the Lutheran Church—Missouri Synod report more than 1000 confirmed members on the roll, but that 5 percent includes one-fourth of all confirmed members. In the Lutheran Church in America one-third of all confirmed members are found in 11 percent of the parishes. Five percent of the congregations in The Mennonite Church account for 23 percent of that denomination's members.

In Canada, where vast area and comparatively sparse population in most parts of the country have produced many small Protestant churches, a similar pattern prevails. Six percent of the congregations in the Presbyterian Church of Canada account for 28 percent of the members. In the United Church of Canada the balance is weighted more toward the middle-sized and smaller congregations than toward the largest congregations which account for 5 percent of all congregations in that denomination and include only 17 percent of the members. In the Baptist Convention of Ontario and Quebec distribution parallels that south of the border as 5 percent of the churches account for one-fourth of the members of the churches in that convention.

What does this mean? Why bring up the fact that a comparatively large proportion of all church members are found in relatively few congregations? Who, besides a few freaks like the author, have any reason to be interested in this statistical phenomenon?

The first and most obvious answer is that statistics tell us where church members are to be found. One-sixth of the congregations account for one-half of all church members! So if the focus of concern is to be on people, large congregations merit a disproportionately large amount of attention.

A second reason for a book on the large church is that larger congregations are different. Many of the common assumptions that apply to the majority of congregations are not relevant to the large church. Whether the subject of the discussion is recruiting lay volunteers or the expectations placed on the minister, the comments and suggestions that are appropriate for the majority of congregations often do not apply to large churches and will turn out to be counterproductive if followed. Large churches display a different pattern of institutional behavior. This is the central theme of the first chapter of this volume.

A third reason is that the criteria and the process for staffing the large church are significantly different from those that are appropriate for most parishes. This is the theme of the second chapter of this volume. Large churches need more staff per 100 members than do middle-sized congregations, which often disturbs those persons who are convinced there is an inherent economy in large scale operations.

A fourth reason for taking a special look at large churches is that they provide a radically different concept for the work of the professional program staff than is to be found in five out of six congregations. The expectations members place upon the ordained staff, the role of lay staff, and the dynamics of interpersonal relationships are different in the large church than in small congregations. Too often a pastor moves from a middle-sized church to become the senior minister of a large congregation and endures some unnecessary hardships because so many people assume that the large church is similar to the middle-sized congregation, only larger. The concept of developing a model for staff relationships, the subject of the third chapter in this volume, is unique to large congregations. It is irrelevant to the needs of the vast majority of churches on the North American continent, but essential to the operation of the large church.

A fifth reason why large churches deserve special attention is found in the imperative of Jesus, "Every one to whom much is given, of him will much be required; and of him to whom men commit much they will demand the more" (Luke 12:48). Denominational leaders, nonchurchgoers, community leaders, members of smaller congregations, and the members of large congregations place heavy demands upon those large churches that obviously have been given much. There are hundreds of large churches, for example, that have given a cumulative total of more than a million dollars to world missions since the close of World War II. Large churches often are seen as the pacesetters in any community or denominational program. They are special, and they merit an examination of their special characteristics, needs, and resources.

Part of the response of scores of large churches to this declaration by our Lord is the development of specialized ministries to the many segments of the population largely ignored in the five out of six churches who focus their evangelistic efforts on that one-third of the adult population who live in households consisting of a husband-wife couple with one or more children under eighteen at home. Many of these family-oriented churches largely ignore other unchurched persons such as young single adults, the handicapped, the exhomemaker, and dozens of other categories. With their unique resources many large churches are developing specialized ministries with persons from this other two-thirds of the adult population.

A sixth reason for a special look at the large church is a result of the emphasis on church growth that emerged during the 1970s. One of the top two or three priorities in the development of any denominational strategy for church growth should be to encourage the continued numerical growth of the larger congregations. This is not an automatic process! Most large churches are staffed for decline. Some are staffed for stability. A few are staffed for growth. As is pointed out in the early part of the second chapter, this is one of the two basic questions to be raised in looking at the staff needs of the large congregation.

A seventh, and perhaps the most subtle reason mentioned here for looking at the distinctive characteristics of the large churches is their role as legitimatizing forces in our culture. By what they do and do not do, large churches exercise a unique role in determining what people will be free to talk about in polite society. They also influence the attitudes and values of millions of people on a variety of subjects ranging from human sexuality to the future of the public schools to the use of alcoholic beverages to church growth to divorce to world hunger to the armaments race. Larger churches are influential molders of public opinion.

An eighth reason for looking at large churches, and a major theme of this book, is that they offer employment for two of the most highly specialized expressions of the professional ministry. The first is the office of the senior minister. The second is the role of the associate minister(s). Most theological seminaries train students to be generalists when they enter the pastoral ministry. Large churches require both generalists and specialists, and often turn out to be the training arena for producing (a) trained and skilled senior pastors and (b) trained and skilled associate ministers. Approximately one-half of this book is devoted to these two highly specialized roles in the pastoral ministry.

Finally, another reason for taking a careful look at the large church can be found in this very disturbing generalization. The larger the organization and/or the greater the emphasis on participatory democracy, the greater the chances that organization will repel the people it is seeking to attract. This generalization applies to singles groups, political parties, educational institutions, and a variety of voluntary organizations as well as to large churches. It means that the organizational structure for planning and decision-making in the large church should not be the same as that used in the small congregation that is governed by a series of congregational meetings and places a great emphasis on participatory democracy. (See items 23 and 24 on pages 26-27).

Before moving on to take a long look at the distinctive characteristics of the large church, it should be emphasized this is not a book in praise of large churches nor a manual on how to find an easy and comfortable life in a large congregation. Everyone, whether a lay volunteer or a professional staff member, should be warned that large congregations are very complex institutions and they offer many uncomfortable moments to the leaders. To be a leader in a large congregation is a hard row to hoe!

Larger congregations provide a unique "behavior setting" for both the paid staff and lay volunteers. Therefore this book begins with a chapter that attempts to identify some of the distinctive characteristics of larger churches.

One of the most complex questions facing leaders of large congregations is providing for an adequate program staff. That issue is the subject of the second chapter and is followed by a chapter describing alternative models for staff relationships and the identification of some neglected factors influencing those relationships. Space does not permit a detailed analysis of the role and responsibilities of each staff member in larger churches, but separate chapters are included on the senior minister and on the associate minister(s). Although they may not approve, most associate ministers will understand why the chapter discussing their role is placed where it is in this book.

The preparation for the writing of this book extends back over the twenty years I have been working as a church planner and parish consultant. I am greatly indebted to the hundreds of larger congregations I have been invited to visit and to the thousands of leaders, both lay and professional, I have met and talked with in those congregations. They have been my instructors for the creation of this book, and I am grateful for the lessons they have taught me.

This volume is dedicated to two outstanding leaders in the church. One recently completed an outstanding career as pastor-counselor-bishop-ecumenist-denominational executive. The other is an articulate and systematic diagnostician, a committed Christian, and an effective lay leader in a large church. I am proud to be able to call them both friends.

CHAPTER ONE
The Large Church

"You're lucky!" exclaimed Harold Haynes as he listened to Linda Rogers describe what was happening in the 1800-member congregation she attended. "My wife and I are members out at Ridgeview where we have fewer than 150 members and we sure have trouble getting enough people to teach in the Sunday school, to fill all the positions on the Board, and to staff all the other offices we need to run a small church with a part-time minister. It must be great to be part of a big church where you have potential leaders running out of your ears. I expect you have more people wanting to hold office than you have places." As she listened with a smile on her face, Linda silently congratulated herself for not laughing at Harold's naive comments.

"The thing I don't understand," reflected Stephen Ross who was in his fourth year as the senior minister at the 2600-member downtown First Church, "is how dependent the people here are on me to initiate new ideas and to give direction. Before coming here I spent nine years as the pastor of an 800-member church in a county seat town. Back there the director of Christian education was the only full-time program staff person besides me. Here I have five full-time and four part-time staff members in program besides myself. We have scores of very gifted laypersons in the membership who are trained, experienced, and highly skilled leaders in their professions and occupations. I doubt if we had a tenth as many really top flight leaders back there as we have here, but back there the lay leaders took the initiative and gave direction to that congregation. I was as much a follower as a leader. Here I sometimes feel I'm the only leader. Everyone else, including my staff, seems to wait for me to take the initiative before they'll express an opinion. Sometimes I feel like I spend all my time trying to lead an army that prefers sitting in the shade and watching me do everything. By contrast, in the church I served before coming here, I felt I was one person in a large cadre of active and creative leaders who were willing to go out on a limb for what we thought God was calling us to do. I guess maybe those folks may have been more committed than are the people here."

"This is the third church in which I've served as the Sunday school superintendent," reflected fifty-five-year-old Woody Carson. "The first was the little country church where I grew up and I was the Sunday school superintendent when I was a senior in high school. Twenty years later I served for three years as the superintendent of a new suburban congregation. When we moved here ten years ago my wife and I decided we would like to see what it would be like to be in a big church, so we joined this 1500-member congregation. Two years ago I was asked to be Sunday school superintendent here. Since I had done it twice before, I thought I'd give it a whirl. I figured that since we have a full-time minister of education, it would be a fairly easy job. You want to know what my biggest problem is? I never would have guessed it or I wouldn't have taken the job. All the teachers want their own room and complete control over it! They don't want anyone else to use it for any purpose during the week. I've never run into that before in my life! Everywhere we've been before no one ever dreamed of having exclusive control of a room to be used only one hour a week. Every room in the building, including the sanctuary, was used by several different groups every week."

These three sets of comments illustrate a very basic, but frequently overlooked point in church planning. Large congregations are substantially different than middle-sized and small churches. If one thinks in terms of institutional behavior patterns, large churches display a different pattern of behavior. These distinctions are of tremendous significance for members of a multiple staff, for lay leaders, and for new members. To move from one church to a congregation of a substantially different size means not only changing addresses and moving into a new set of interpersonal relationships, it also means moving into an arena where the institutional behavior of the congregation is different. Big churches are not only larger, they are different.

What Are the Differences?

Perhaps the best approach to identifying some of these differences is to go back to the three persons at the beginning of this chapter, describe what was behind their comments, and thus build a list of the differences which set the large church apart from other congregations.

1. Perhaps the most widely held misconception about large congregations is that they are enjoying a plethora of leadership. This usually is an illusion in the eye of the observer from a smaller church. The safe assumption is that the larger the membership, the easier it is for a member to respond negatively to a request to accept a position as a lay volunteer. The larger the congregation, the more difficult it is to enlist lay volunteers. The larger the congregation, the greater the degree of persistence that is required of those responsible for recruiting lay volunteers. Why? Part of the response to that one-word question is that the larger the membership, the easier it is for a member to assume there is someone else who is better qualified, or more competent, and who has a more flexible schedule to accept that responsibility. Therefore, the potential lay volunteer can respond honestly and sincerely by saying, "I'm sure you can find someone else who would be able to do a better job than I could do; why don't you ask them?"

By contrast, in the small church the members who are asked to accept positions of responsibility know that if they respond negatively there is a good chance the positions will remain vacant. Furthermore, in the small or middle-sized church there is a high probability that the person making the request is a friend, relative, hard-working fellow member, or someone with a close personal relationship to the one being asked. It is more difficult to turn down a friend or relative than it is to respond negatively to an acquaintance, a stranger, or a staff member "who is getting paid to do that, so why should I volunteer to help him do what we're paying him to do?"

In addition, the larger the congregation, the larger the proportion of members who feel they are outside that inner "fellowship circle" and therefore do not have to accept the responsibilities of being a lay volunteer.

Finally, the larger the congregation the greater the probability that lay volunteers will be exploited without adequate appreciation, rather than reinforced with appropriate expressions of support and gratitude.[1]

2. One of the basic differences between the dynamics of small groups and the functioning of large groups is that the larger the number of persons in the group, the greater the demands the collection of people place on the leadership to initiate. In a small group the responsibility for initiating new ideas or for giving direction rests largely with the group. As the size of the group increases, members gradually shift this responsibility to the leadership and expect the leaders to accept the role of initiator.[2]

This concept can be illustrated in pastor-congregation relationships by looking at the journey of one minister who began his career in a long-established, stable, small, rural church. There the minister was the "preacher." A few years later, after a move to a slightly larger, but also very stable congregation, that same minister functioned as a "facilitator," or "enabler." His third position was in a larger county seat town where he was comfortable as "a leader among leaders." His fourth step was to become the senior minister of a very large church where everyone expected the senior minister to be *the* leader. Each move brought a change in the role of the minister as the size of the congregation changed.

The vast majority of members of the large church expect the senior minister to be a directive and initiating leader. The basic variable is whether that initiating responsibility will be vested in (1) the office of the senior minister or (2) the professional program staff or (3) the senior minister and three or four lay leaders or (4) a small group of leaders composed of the senior minister, one or two other staff members, and two or three lay leaders.

The fifth and sixth alternatives of either expecting the governing body of the congregation to be the initiating group or of leaving that responsibility unfulfilled usually produce large quantities of frustration.

In other words, Stephen Ross' experience as the senior minister of the 2600-member First Church was not different because the members were less dedicated than the members of his former parish. It was different because First Church was more than four times as large as the congregation he had served earlier. The larger the congregation, the greater the expectations that institution places on the senior minister to be the initiating leader. Black pastors and white pastors of large independent congregations tend to be more willing to accept this leadership role than are many white senior ministers in the mainline predominantly white denominational churches.

3. A common pattern of institutional behavior was experienced by Woody Carson and can be described in one sentence. The larger the congregation, the greater the conflict over use of rooms and the greater the volume of complaints that "somebody has been using our room." This is a simple descriptive statement. Why it happens moves the discussion to a level of speculation. One reason appears to be that as the size of the group increases, the desire for privacy and control of one's own "turf" also rises. That pattern of institutional behavior can be seen in many organizations. In the large church, perhaps control of one's own room offsets the lack of appreciation received by teachers. Undoubtedly another reason is that the larger the congregation, the greater the attachment of the typical member to a subgroup such as a Sunday school class or the women's organization and the more limited the sense of belonging to the larger organization. Therefore, "our room" has a unique role in reinforcing the distinctive identity of that

subgroup. Obviously the larger congregations often can afford the luxury of specialized rooms while most smaller churches have no choice but multiple use of space. In the larger churches people therefore expect specialized uses of facilities, and when that expectation is not fulfilled, one result is tension.

4. While it overlaps the first three on this list of distinctions, a fourth difference is that the larger the congregation, the more critical the need for a systematic and intentional system for the development and maintenance of a network of lay volunteers. In the small church the members spontaneously do this. In the middle-sized congregation this responsibility may be carried by the pastor or by a lay volunteer. In the larger congregation it usually requires considerable time from one staff person. In the huge congregations the development and care of a network of lay volunteers often requires all of one staff member's time plus the investment of time and energy by other staff persons with the assistance of several lay volunteers.

In other words, the larger the congregation, the more important and also the more complicated the system for caring for the network of lay volunteers and the greater the responsibility of the paid staff for this concern.

5. The larger the congregation, the more important the need on Sunday morning for convenient off-street parking spaces for visitors and potential new members.

Larger congregations usually meet in complex buildings without a clearly defined "main entrance." The best answer is to reserve parking spaces for visitors near the correct entrance. This is unnecessary in the majority of churches.

6. The larger the congregation, the more important it is for all members to wear nametags every Sunday morning. One reason is to help members know one another by name. A second reason is to help members identify and welcome visitors. A third reason is that name tags have important symbolic value. They symbolize the acceptance of the fact that this is a large congregation that expects strangers to be present every Sunday, and the regular use of nametags represents a "Welcome, stranger! This-is-my-name" attitude by the members.

7. The larger the congregation, the more necessary it is to plan for the care of the members rather than assume it will happen spontaneously.

In the majority of Protestant congregations on the North American continent an informal system operates to help members be aware of births and deaths, to remember birthdays and wedding anniversaries, to welcome and assimilate new members, to lift up the departure of members who are moving away, and to highlight other important events in the lives of members. By contrast, in the larger congregations these events will pass unnoticed by most members unless an intentional effort is made to keep everyone informed.

8. The larger the congregation, the more important it is to have a carefully designed, systematic, and highly redundant internal communication system.

In the larger congregations the majority of messages from the church to the members are not received or at least not received and remembered. A greater degree of redundancy, therefore, is required to achieve an acceptable level of internal communication.[3]

9. The larger the congregation, the greater the temptation for many leaders to "play house" and to focus on real estate concerns rather than to grapple with questions of purpose, role, and mission.

The reasons for this tendency can be found in the fact that the larger the congregation the more likely (a) its community identity is based to a substantial extent on the meeting place; (b) it is difficult for any one leader to fully comprehend the entire range of ministries and programs carried on by the church, and therefore it is tempting to focus on the more visible real estate concerns; and (c) the size of the financial investment in the meeting place will be a very impressive figure, and the amount of money devoted to maintaining that meeting place also will be a substantial figure.

10. The larger the congregation, the more vulnerable that church is to unexpected changes.

Large churches tend to be comparatively fragile and lack the stability of small congregations. A common expression of this is in the major fluctuations in worship attendance, Sunday school attendance, and other forms of lay participation over a relatively brief span of years.

This is most likely to occur with a change in the senior minister or with changes in the community context and often is accompanied by a rapid turnover in the lay leadership.

By contrast, small churches frequently show only modest changes in membership, attendance, participation, and lay leadership as pastors come and go or as the residents of the surrounding community move away or die and are replaced. In other words, the larger the congregation, the more vulnerable it is to change.

11. The larger the congregation, the more disruptive are changes in the professional staff.

This generalization overlaps item 10 and is one of several generalizations, including items 2 and 4 from this list, directed specifically at larger churches that have a multiple staff.

It is much more difficult to build a closely knit and complementary program staff that matches the personality and needs of the large congregation than it is to find a pastor for a smaller church. Thus when the membership of the staff is altered, the result is likely to be very disruptive and occasionally causes people to choose sides over the change.

12. The larger the congregation, the more disruptive the shock that accompanies any radical change in the leadership style of the senior minister due to a change of pastors.

The corollary to this is that in congregations with one minister and no other program staff, the role and duties of the pastor usually are rather clearly and sometimes even rigidly defined. Thus, in smaller churches a new minister, regardless of leadership style, has to make some adaptation to the role as it exists.

By contrast, the larger the staff, the less clearly and the less firmly defined are the role and duties of each individual staff member. (See items 2, and 15–19 for additional implications.)

13. The larger the congregation, the more important it becomes for everyone, and especially for the senior minister, to recognize and accept the fact that the senior minister cannot be *the* shepherd, or pastor, to *every* member.

14. The larger the professional staff, the more likely there will be

confusion over who a particular member will turn to as *my* pastor in time of personal or family crisis.

In the typical large multiple-staff congregation most members view the senior minister as "my pastor," but many turn to one of the other ministers for that role or to the director of Christian education, the minister of music, or to some other staff member to be their shepherd, advisor, or pastor. This cannot happen in smaller churches where there is only one staff person, except perhaps for those members who continue to view the predecessor as "our pastor."

15. The larger the congregation, the greater the dependence for stability and continuity on (a) the staff and (b) the group life of the church during times of stress, tension, uncertainty, or external change, *but* the greater the temptation to build the congregation around the magnetic personality of one staff member, usually the senior minister.

Every congregation, regardless of size, tends to depend on the same general factors (the minister, the meeting place, the interpersonal relationships among the members, the shared experiences from the past, the subgroups in that church, a distinctive missional thrust, the theological stance, the denominational affiliation, the package of program and ministries, the decision-making structures, or the lay leadership) to maintain a sense of continuity. The big difference is that in the smaller churches some of these, such as the meeting place, the Sunday school, and the shared experiences from the past, are especially important. By contrast, in the larger churches that sense of continuity usually is much more dependent on the minister, the subgroups, and the paid staff. This helps explain, for example, why it is often comparatively easy for the large church with a long tenure senior minister to display considerable hostility toward the denomination or even to leave that denomination. Many very large congregations function as minidenominations and do not need the denominational label for a sense of continuity.

16. The larger the congregation, the more disruptive is the change when one minister replaces another on the staff.

This is especially true whenever there is a change in senior ministers. The basic reasons for this can be found in the previous sections of this chapter. The larger the congregation, the more dependent it is on the staff for pace, direction, and a sense of institutional identity.

17. The larger the congregation, the more important it is to encourage long pastorates.

Pastoral changes usually are disruptive, but often are especially disruptive in very large congregations.

The basic exceptions to this generalization are (a) when there is a poor match between minister and congregation (see item 19 below), (b) when the basic continuity of the congregation is in lay-controlled group life (such as the adult Sunday school classes and/or the women's organization and/or lay-led Bible study and prayer groups), (c) when that congregation has a distinctive theological stance that sets it apart from all other religious congregations in the community (examples of this include the Mormons, the Seventh Day Adventists, and the Seventh Day Baptists), (d) when the crucial continuity in the staff is not with the ordained ministers but rather is vested in a lay staff member (choir director, director of Christian education, parish worker, etc.) who has long tenure and who has developed a large program or ministry with a tremendous amount of lay participation and support. (Critics of such programs often point out that "the tail is wagging the dog here.")

18. The larger the congregation and the longer it has been in existence, the more complex the requirements of the staff.

This difference helps explain why it usually takes longer and is a more complicated task to find a replacement for a program staff member in the large congregation than to find a new minister for a smaller congregation.

The basic reason for this is that the role of a staff member, including the role of the senior minister, usually is less clearly structured in the larger churches. That role also is shaped by the personalities, gifts, interests, and skills of the persons who fill the other staff positions.

When this factor is ignored in filling the position of associate minister, the most common result is a short tenure for the new associate.

This factor also is one reason why many large churches are replacing the full-time associate minister, who often is a generalist, with two or three part-time lay specialists, each with a precisely defined role and task such as parish visitor, leadership development specialist, youth director, choir director, or director of ministry with single adults. This change often simplifies role definition and facilitates the supervisory responsibility of the senior minister.

19. The larger the congregation, the more vulnerable that church is to an inappropriate match of pastor and people.

One reason for this is that large churches are unusually dependent on the pastor. A second reason is that large churches need long pastorates. A third reason, as pointed out in the previous section, is that in large churches the role of the pastor often is less clearly structured. A fourth reason is that large churches are more fragile institutions as contrasted to small churches which usually are tougher and more resilient.

20. The larger the congregation, the greater the institutional pressure on the senior minister to place a higher priority on administration rather than on spending time with members in a pastoral role.

The over-arching generalization behind this distinction is that the larger the institution, the more likely it is that the institution will control the actions of the person holding a major office, rather than the holder of that office controlling the institution. Every President since Harry Truman has commented on that pattern. The parallel is that the larger the congregation, and the longer it has been in existence *as a large church,* the less discretion the senior minister has over his or her allocation of time and energy and the greater the premium the lay leaders place on the administrative skills of the holder of the office of senior minister.

A widespread response to this pattern of institutional behavior is to employ a church business administrator in an effort to free the senior minister to spend more time on preaching, pastoral care, and other ministerial duties. Occasionally this response turns out to be a good solution to the problem.

21. The larger the congregation, the greater the probability that when a member, who regularly attends one particular service on Sunday morning, comes at a different hour, he or she will feel like a stranger or a visitor rather than a member.

One response to this distinctive characteristic of the large church is to deplore it. Another is to minimize choices and offer only one Sunday morning worship experience. A third, that is no more productive than the first two, is to encourage members to vary their own schedules instead of attending at the same hour. A fourth, and far more productive response, is to forget about trying to be "one big happy family" and affirm the fact that the large church is really a congregation of congregations which must, as a function of its size, offer meaningful choices to people.

22. The larger the congregation, the more crucial it is in program planning to use *both* the small group model and the large group model in program development.

Large group events, ranging in size from thirty-five to several hundred, are an essential element in the program planning for large churches. The large church that persists in planning program development solely or largely around a small group model usually will not grow, frequently requires a much larger professional staff, usually has a disproportionately large number of inactive members, and only rarely can meet all the needs of even a majority of the members.

23. The larger the congregation, the greater the need for an organizational and decision-making structure that emphasizes performance.

Small and middle-sized churches can function reasonably effectively with an organizational structure based on representation and/or participation of a large proportion of the members in the decision-making processes. By contrast, however, the large church requires a radically different organizational structure which is designed to facilitate the making and implementation of decisions. In other words, a 50 or 80 or 90-member governing body may provide more advantages than disadvantages in the 300-member congregation, but it is a counterproductive model in the large congregation where it usually is necessary to (a) limit the size of the governing body to fewer than two dozen members or (b) create an executive committee if the governing body has more than two dozen members in order to be able to legislate and to implement or (c) cheerfully affirm the fact that "the senior minister really runs the church, and we watch and agree with what he does" or (d) develop some creative response to the frustration created when decisions are not made, or, if they are made, not implemented.

24. The larger the congregation, the greater the need for carefully disciplined planning and preparation of every event and program.

The members of smaller congregations often are more tolerant and more accepting of ad hoc, "off-the-cuff," presentations and usually are willing to tolerate poorly planned programs. As the size of the congregation increases, however, that toleration begins to erode. The larger the congregation, the less tolerance for sloppy performances, for inadequately planned events, for unnecessary schedule conflicts, for inept communication, for poorly maintained physical facilities, for low quality musical programs and for departures from agreed-upon schedules and expectations.

This is not offered as a complete list of the distinctive characteristics that set the large churches apart from the smaller congregations. This list is included only to illustrate that large churches, and especially those with a multiple staff, display a different pattern of institutional behavior than do smaller churches.

What Is a Large Church?

When it comes to defining the term "large church" a variety of alternatives come to mind. A simple dividing line would be to refer to the one Protestant congregation in twenty that reports more than a thousand confirmed members as a large church. A parallel, but more inclusive approach would be to define as large churches those that average more than two hundred at worship on the Sabbath. This second definition expands the list to about 15 percent of all Protestant congregations on the continent. It would be consistent with the basic thrust of this book to define as large churches those that employ two or more persons in program staff positions. Each of these definitions has value, but there is another alternative.

While it is more complicated, a better approach begins with the recognition that such categories as "small" or "middle-sized" or "large" are inadequate in classifying churches on the basis of size.[4] If one accepts the basic assumption made here that size influences the patterns of institutional behavior of churches, then it may be useful to use a more elaborate set of categories. This requires a different yardstick than membership for measuring size. The definition of who is reported as a "member" varies not only from congregation to congregation within the same denomination, but even more across denominational lines. A better, more accurate and less flexible yardstick in measuring the size of a congregation is to use average attendance at worship. For the churches with two or more worship services on Sunday morning this refers to the combined attendance for all services. The accompanying table shows seven categories ofcongregations based on size as determined by the average attendance at worship. In each category one size is listed to identify the average

CLASSIFYING CHURCHES BY SIZE

Average Attendance at Worship	Percentile	Type
35	25%	Fellowship
75	50%	Small
140	75%	Middle-sized
200	85%	Awkward size
350	95%	Large
600	98%	Huge
700 or more	100%	Minidenomination

attendance at worship for a congregation of that type. This is followed by a percentile figure to show where that size congregation ranks when compared to all other Protestant congregations on the continent. Thus the typical "middle-sized" congregation averages around 140 at worship and that means it is larger than three-quarters of all other Protestant congregations in the United States and Canada.

When this system is used, the largest single category of churches turns out to be the fellowships. These are the congregations that average less than 35 to 40 at Sunday morning worship, and they account for approximately 30 percent of all churches. (In the United Methodist Church, for example, one-third of all congregations report an average attendance of 42 or less at the principal weekly worship service.) These congregations can be described as fellowships. They resemble an overgrown small group, with a strong emphasis on the relationships of the members to one another. These fellowships usually are controlled by the laity, rather than the clergy, and offer the largest number of examples of the ministry of the laity that can be found anywhere on the religious scene in North America. Usually neither the members nor the denomination expect this type congregation to carry out all the functions of the typical church in terms of program, outreach, staffing, or participation in denominational activities. This size and type of church usually comes closer than any other category of church in offering the spontaneous caring for one another that is described in the New Testament.

Another 20–30 percent of all Protestant congregations can be grouped together as "small churches." Typically they average between 50 and 100 at worship, and many of them are able to secure the services of a full-time pastor. Frequently this size church provides a compensation package for the pastor that, when translated into dollars, averages out to three or four dollars per member per week. In many respects this size congregation offers many advantages and benefits, and comparatively few disadvantages to the members and as a result usually includes a relatively small proportion of inactive members.[5]

The middle-sized congregation averages between 100 and 175 at worship and frequently has a full-time resident pastor. In many respects, the congregation averaging 125 to 175 at worship represents the optimum size church. It usually has an adequate number of lay leaders who possess a variety of gifts and talents. This size congregation usually can both afford and justify a full-time pastor and perhaps a part-time secretary. On a per member basis the congregation averaging 160 to 170 at worship usually has the lowest costs for paid staff of any size church. This size congregation usually can offer several choices to the members in program, ministries, and opportunities for meaningful participation. In most cases it can maintain an adequate meeting place without real estate becoming a burdensome distraction from ministry. The resources are available for it to be actively and meaningfully involved in outreach and mission, and it usually has enough strength to develop one or two specialized ministries to persons who may be overlooked by other churches in the community, but it is still small enough for the members to know one another and for much of the ministry of the church to be initiated spontaneously. Slightly more than one-fifth of all Protestant congregations average between 100 and 175 at worship.

From a ministerial perspective this also is the largest size congregation in which the pastor can function effectively with the enabler leadership style. This is not to suggest that the enabler style is the ideal style for the pastor of a middle-size church. The enabler style of leadership is the most demanding of any ministerial leadership role and requires a remarkably high level of competence in many different areas. It is unreasonable to expect more than a tiny proportion of ministers to have that level of competence in so many different areas of responsibility and skill.

For the minister who does have that remarkable assortment of gifts, however, the middle-sized church is the ideal place to serve. By contrast, the minister serving as the pastor of a larger congregation must be more of an initiating leader, more directive, more self-reliant, more willing to act as the "chief of staff" of a large organization, more comfortable with "command" responsibilities and at least somewhat uncomfortable with the Carl Rogers school of humanistic psychology.[6]

The next size bracket averages between 175 and 225 at worship. This often is an awkward and uncomfortable size *from the perspective of the pastor,* although many of the members find it to be a very comfortable size church. While it has most of the advantages of the congregation averaging 150 at worship, it usually is too large to be served adequately by one full-time program staff member, but frequently is too small for the members to believe they both need and can afford additional program staff. Sometimes this pressure is relieved by providing an exceptionally competent full-time church secretary who also is in fact the administrative assistant to the minister, the hub of the internal communications network, and the office manager. This size congregation, except for those that are less than ten years old and also have retained their original momentum for growth, usually is too large to expect to grow without adding program staff, but often feels it cannot afford more staff. That is one reason why it is an "awkward size." A second reason is that it usually is too large to be able to offer a meaningful worship experience for everyone by scheduling only one service on Sunday morning, but the members often resist the idea of offering two services. It is too large to function as one congregation, but too small for the members to recognize, accept, and affirm the idea of seeing themselves as a congregation of congregations. One result is a growing proportion of relatively inactive members. Another result is that congregations of this type find it very difficult to make changes because many members find their plateau so comfortable they oppose change.

The term "large church" can be applied to those congregations that average between 225 and 450 at worship. Approximately one Protestant congregation in ten fits into this bracket. It differs from smaller congregations in several respects. Typically it has two or three full-time (or the equivalent in part-time positions) program staff, in addition to secretarial, bookkeeping and custodial employees. More often than not, this size congregation offers two or three worship experiences on Sunday morning. It usually functions as a congregation of congregations of groups, classes, circles, and organizations *unless it is a relatively new and unusually homogeneous congregation.* Normally everyone agrees that a redundant internal communication system is necessary and this usually includes a weekly newsletter to the members. Frequently, this size congregation has a systematic lay training program to nurture that network of lay volunteers which does not maintain itself automatically. Because of its size and the diversity there usually is some conflict among the staff and/or among the members over what God is calling the congregation to be and to do and on what the priorities should be in the allocation of financial resources. This size congregation usually has sufficient leadership, both in paid staff and from among lay volunteers, that it is conspicuously represented in community affairs and/or denominational activities. It also is large enough to operate three or four or more specialized ministries such as a weekday nursery school, a drama group, a day care center, a special ministry to mature adults, a ministry to handicapped persons, a huge youth program, a youth choir that goes on tour every year, a ministry with single adults, a camping program or a special missionary outreach project. In those congregations which only recently have grown into this size bracket there often is some confusion or tension because the roles of the individual staff members have not yet been institutionalized.

While the reasons are in the realm of speculation, this size congregation often appears to have difficulty breaking the barrier that appears to emerge when it reaches the 450 attendance mark. If congregations are classified by membership figures, there appears to be a slightly larger number than membership figures would suggest in the 300 to 450 worship range and fewer than would be expected in the 450 to 600 worship-attendance bracket. In other words, it appears that while some large congregations continue to grow in terms of reported membership, they reach a plateau in worship attendance and level out at the 350 to 450 attendance bracket.

One reason, as suggested in the next chapter, is that many large churches are staffed for remaining on a plateau and not for growth. Another reason is that the congregation averaging 500 to 700 at worship is a substantially different type church. This usually means that for the church averaging 350 to 450 at worship to grow to 600 or more at worship requires a change in how the members see themselves as a congregation, a change in the leadership role of the senior minister, a change in the organizational and decision-making structure to place a greater emphasis on performance (usually at the cost of a decrease in representation and participation), and a change in how the leaders conceptualize the program. That's a lot of change, so frequently a congregation will level out with a worship attendance in the 350 to 450 bracket rather than make the changes that would enable it to move off the plateau.

The next bracket, when churches are classified by attendance, consists of the estimated 6,000 Protestant congregations averaging 450 to 700 at worship. These can be described as "huge" churches.

The typical huge congregation has a long history of a multiple staff, and members understand and accept the need for a comparatively large paid staff. Denominational leaders, pastors, and members of other congregations look to the huge church as a pacesetting leader in both denominational and community affairs. A large proportion of these huge churches have contributed a cumulative total of a million dollars or more to benevolences during the past quarter century and are viewed by the denomination as basic sources of financial support for special needs. The members of the typical huge church usually have accepted both the advantages and the anonymity that often are a function of size. Specialization is a part of the way of life of the huge church and this applies both to the paid staff and to many of the lay volunteers. The typical huge congregation is a well-organized operation, and administration usually consumes a large proportion of the time and energy of the senior minister, although these pressures may be reduced by employing a church business administrator. This size congregation usually has at least two full-time ordained ministers on the staff and those that have a strong growth orientation usually employ three or four ordained members, one or two of whom specialize in education, music, program development, evangelism, or youth or community ministries.

33

Only one Protestant congregation in a hundred averages more than 700 at worship, and this is one of two categories where independent or nondenominational churches show up in disproportionately large numbers. (The other is small fellowships.) These congregations, *if they sustain that size over a long period of time,* can be described as "minidenominations." Some observers refer to them as "super-churches." This size congregation often performs on a unilateral basis many of the functions usually shared on a denominational basis. Examples include operating their own camp or retreat center, preparing their own educational and/or confirmation curriculum, conducting their own lay leadership development programs, operating their own special home mission projects, sponsoring several foreign missionaries, operating their own weekday school, offering continuing education events for clergy, and sponsoring the organization of new congregations. The typical mini-denomination church often is criticized as resembling a big business with its elaborate plans, high visibility, huge budget, heavy dependence on paid staff, large and complex building, receptionists, computers, weekly television program and/or daily radio broadcast, variety of ministries, carefully organized decision-making structure and attractively printed public relations materials.

One reason for this criticism is that the mini-denomination church is a big business. The total annual receipts usually range between one-half million and five million dollars. The annual contributions to missions by the average mini-denomination church usually exceeds the total income of nine out of ten churches. The mini-denomination church deals in awesome figures.

In reviewing these seven categories of churches by size it is important to remember the two basic reasons for the use of this system of classification. First, the size of a congregation influences its institutional behavior. The large, huge, and mini-denomination churches display different patterns of institutional behavior than do smaller congregations.

Second, each size category provides a different "behavior setting" for both the members and the staff.[7] Research in ecological psychology reveals that people tend to conform to the standing patterns of the behavior settings in which they find themselves. In other words, the minister who served for six years as the pastor of a small church will function differently when she moves to become the associate minister of a large church. That new behavior setting will create a different set of social inputs, and she will respond to these new social inputs in a manner that will change her behavior patterns from what they were in the small church. Failure to recognize the impact of behavior settings is one of the major sources of tension and of unfulfilled expectations in multiple staff churches.

Perhaps the best way to illustrate how the behavior setting influences congregational life is to focus in on one narrowly defined function of congregational life in four different size churches.

Who Greets the Strangers?

What happens when a stranger comes alone to worship with a congregation that he or she has never visited before? In the fellowship church the members frequently are a little surprised, they are not used to visitors, but everyone is aware of the visitor and most of the members take the initiative to greet the stranger. The entire process of recognition and greeting is very informal and unplanned. It also should be noted that a visitor who is not accompanied by a member often is a disruptive element in the fellowship church, simply because a stranger in that type of behavior setting stands out very prominently.

By contrast, the middle-sized congregation often is expecting strangers and in response to that expectation has defined a role to be filled by a member. Typically the person filling that role is called an usher and the usher usually (a) greets each person entering the sanctuary, (b) escorts each person to a place to sit, (c) hands that person a bulletin and, depending on the traditions of that particular congregation, may (d) help in receiving the Sunday morning offering, help serve the Lord's Supper on Communion Sunday, escort people from their pew after the benediction, collect prayer requests from people when they enter and deliver them to the pastor, respond to any emergencies that may arise, invite visitors to sign the guest register, and/or respond to questions.

The larger churches, as a result of their greater size and complexity, often create a different behavior setting. Frequently this behavior setting includes the expectation that strangers will be present every Sunday morning, so a new role may be created to be filled by lay volunteers. This is the role of information giver or of information giver *and* receiver. In one church this role is filled by the person who wears the ASK ME badge every Sunday morning. This responsibil-

ity usually is rotated among several persons, each of whom is knowledgeable about the total life, program, and ministry of the congregation. The person filling that role is expected to arrive 20 to 30 minutes early, to greet the people coming to the first worship service and, later, to greet those coming to church school, to initiate conversations with strangers who may have questions, to be highly visible and available during the Sunday school hour, to greet the early arrivals for the second or third worship service, to record the name and address of every visitor, and to circulate among those who stay for the coffee hour following the worship service. This 3 to 4½ hour tour of duty is best filled by a knowledgeable, extroverted, outgoing, and gregarious individual. Unlike the ushers, who may spend most of their time with members, the information givers spend most of their time with visitors.

Other churches respond to this need by staffing an informational table near the main entrance. This means that in some buildings two or three tables are necessary because there is not a single heavily used entrance. A common pattern is to have one person serve as the principle resource person at the same table for several months. This resource person is available to answer questions, give directions to visitors, distribute literature, provide a nametag for each visitor, help wives find missing husbands or children, add names to the church's mailing list, and receive suggestions. In the larger congregations this individual may be assisted by two or three persons who will escort strangers to the appropriate Sunday school room, introduce visitors to leaders, guide visitors through the building, and also assist the principal host or hostess when the volume of requests peak.

The larger the congregation and/or the more complex the building and/or the larger the number of visitors and/or the greater the emphasis on welcoming strangers, the more important is the staffing of this informational role. Several congregations that place a high priority on welcoming visitors have both the information tables approach and two or three people with ASK ME badges circulating around the building. This would be perceived as incongruous in the typical small church where the behavior setting calls for a less structured and more informal response to strangers.

As the size of the congregation increases, the behavior setting usually becomes more complex and there is a greater chance of overlooking a visitor. A useful response to this increased complexity is to build a greater degree of redundancy into the system for greeting strangers. This can be achieved by creating a third role, that of greeter. Unlike the ushers, who usually meet people at a door leading into the nave, the greeters often meet people at a door leading into the building and, in pleasant weather, may greet people outside the building or out in the parking lot.

The most important single responsibility of the greeter is to extend a warm welcome to the stranger. The second responsibility of the greeter is to learn, remember, and record the name and address of each visitor. This is especially critical in those congregations which seek to welcome the growing number of "church shoppers." When a visitor returns for the second time and is greeted by name, this surprise almost inevitably produces the feeling "this church really cares about people." This tends to happen only when each greeter (a) is successful in learning and remembering the names of strangers, (b) is on the alert to spot return visits from persons who have been there once or twice before, (c) is involved in sharing with other greeters the names and descriptions of visitors, (d) is part of a permanent team of trained, outgoing, and gregarious persons who function as a team that enjoys its joint responsibility, rather than as a member of a group with a rotating membership that requires each greeter to be on duty only once a month or once a quarter, and (e) is a member of a congregation in which the leaders have elevated the role of greeter to one of the highest priorities in assigning lay volunteers. This process is reinforced when everyone, including both members and visitors, is encouraged to wear a nametag. Several churches also offer courses in the art of remembering names to all greeters.

A fairly common sequence is for the greeter to identify, greet, meet and learn the name of a visitor. After a minute or two of getting acquainted, this gregarious greeter escorts the visitor over to an usher and introduces the visitor to the usher and the usher to the visitor. After writing down the name, address, and other information about that visitor(s), the greeter leaves this new friend with the usher and returns to welcome other newcomers. This sequence obviously means that in those churches that expect and welcome strangers, it usually will be necessary to have a team of greeters rather than only one or two. It also means that all members recognize and accept a system of priorities that places welcoming strangers and visitors at the top of the list and visits by the greeter with longtime members and old friends at the bottom of the list.

A major benefit of this system of responsibilities for greeters is that it produces the names, addresses, and descriptive data of each visitor so that a personal visit may be made to that visitor within 72 hours. If visits are not made or if a letter or telephone call is used to replace a personal visit, this tends to reduce the value of an effective system of greeters. In several congregations the understanding with each greeter is that he or she will make a personal visit to each visitor he or she met on Sunday morning. This reinforces the relationship between the greeter and the visitor and makes it easier for the greeter to recognize that visitor the following Sunday.

In several huge and mini-denomination size congregations where the behavior setting places a premium on identifying and welcoming visitors a system is used that would be completely unacceptable in most small churches. This calls for the ushers to guide all visitors to the door where the senior minister is greeting people. In some churches the pastor's secretary stands nearby and takes down in shorthand all relevant comments and types them up before leaving. This provides names, addresses, and other details for followup calls on the visitors.

In each of the examples described here the behavior setting calls for different systems for greeting strangers and creates a variety of different roles for both laity and clergy. What would be appropriate, acceptable, and effective in one behavior setting will be perceived as inappropriate and unacceptable in another setting. The size of the congregation influences the nature of the behavior setting, which influences how the members will respond to a specific question, need, or problem.

Clan, Tribe, or Nation?

Another useful frame of reference in describing how large churches differ from middle-sized and small congregations is to use the anthropological analogy of the tribe.

Every tribe uses a variety of symbols to enable both members and nonmembers to identify who is a member of a particular tribe. Every tribe has its own rites for initiating new members into the tribe. Every tribe has a series of symbols and rituals that are used to preserve and celebrate the history of that collection of people. Every tribe has its own distinctive identity.

This concept can be illustrated by reviewing the distinctive characteristics of Israel's early organizational structure which included four subdivisions: nation, tribe, clan, and household (Joshua 7:16-18). Sometimes a clan grew to the point that it divided as did Joseph's. Some tribes grew large and strong while others dwindled and disappeared. Frequently the corporate identity of the tribe was in its leader.

In the history of the New Testament church it soon became necessary for the called-out community to develop a distinctive identity. The first great council meeting of the churches (Acts 15) was called to clarify the essential initiatory rites for a person to become a member of that called-out community. Baptism and the Lord's Supper have been defined by most Christian communities as two essential rites. As the centuries passed Christian churches adopted a large number and a large variety of what can be described very simply as tribal customs. These include uniforms for the clergy, distinctive names for clans, tribes, and nations, requirements for admission into membership, symbols and seals, songs and artifacts, the veneration of saints and martyrs, distinctive meeting places, distinctive dress for members of a specific order of religious vocations, elaborate installation services for important tribal leaders, the codification of the rules of tribal organization, extensive tribal histories, and the celebration of the historic anniversaries of the tribe.

A similar thread can be seen in American Indian tribes, adult Sunday school classes, universities, lodges, governments, athletic teams, service clubs, fraternities, sororities, African tribes, labor unions, Scouting, professional and academic societies, the United States Senate, the women's organizations in the churches, the United Nations, insurance companies, councils of churches, military organizations, and theological seminaries. Each of these can be understood in institutional terms by viewing it as a tribe. As the years pass it accumulates a growing number of tribal customs, rites, rituals, symbols, anniversaries, legends, and traditions that reinforce a sense of belonging among the members of the tribe.

When this frame of reference is used in looking at churches by size, the fellowship church resembles the family, the small church resembles the clan, the large church resembles the tribe, and the huge church, especially the minidenomination, begins to resemble a nation. Why does the church averaging a thousand or more at worship often appear to outsiders to be a minidenomination? Because it is too large to function as a tribe among other smaller tribes, it is more like a nation of tribes. Or, to translate that into ecclesiastical language, while the large church often resembles a congregation of congrega-

tions of groups, classes, circles, and organizations, the minidenomination may function more like a denomination of congregations each
with its own overlapping subgroups.

What's the point of this analogy?

There are at least five reasons why it is a useful analogy in studying
the unique characteristics of congregations with a multiple staff.

The first reason for using the tribal analogy is to emphasize the
unique role of the pastor of the very large church. In the smaller
congregations the role of the patriarch, or tribal chief, usually is filled
by an older lay person. The minister is the visiting medicine man.
Tribal identity is in the laity, not in the pastor.

By contrast, in congregations with a multiple staff, and especially
the huge and mini-denomination size churches, the role of the tribal
chief often is filled by the senior minister. Frequently the corporate
identity of the very large church is in the personality of the senior
minister who has served that congregation for a decade or longer. The
senior minister is the patriarch,, the tribal chief, and the number one
medicine man. A simple illustration is when the recently arrived
twenty-six-year-old assistant medicine man visits an elderly member
in the hospital and is asked, "When is the number one medicine man
coming to see me?" A second illustration of this distinction is that
even a year or two after arriving, the pastor of the small church often is
perceived as "our new preacher." In contrast, considerably more
deference is accorded the new senior minister of the huge church. The
office of tribal chief ranks considerably higher in the tribal pecking
order than does the position of itinerant medicine man. This also helps
explain why the departure of the senior minister from the very large
congregation usually produces more disruption than when the
minister of the small church moves to another congregation.

A second reason for lifting up this analogy is that it illustrates why
larger churches often have difficulty in assimilating new members.
The basic generalization is that the larger the congregation or the
longer it has been in existence, the more important it is to develop a
redundant system for initiating new members into the tribe and
helping them gain a sense of belonging. Too often, however, the same

basic system of receiving new members is used in the very large congregations as is used in much smaller churches. Some large congregations recognize the importance of tribal symbols and present each new member with a key to the front door of the church, a lapel pin, or some other distinctive symbol when a person is received into membership. Likewise the larger the congregation, the more important it is to have a series of classes for new members to help them learn the distinctive history and to become acquainted with the folklore of that tribe.

A third factor is that the larger the tribe, the more dependent the members are on symbols, traditions, legends, celebrations, rituals, songs, and other tribal events for maintaining a sense of tribal unity. In other words, the larger the congregation, the more helpful it is in enhancing the sense of unity, cohesiveness, and belonging to have a distinctive name for that congregation, to celebrate anniversaries, to publish the church history, to provide a unique "uniform" (the contemporary translation of that concept is a distinctive T-shirt) for the youth group, to provide directories with photographs of every member of the tribe, to develop a distinctive symbol or logo symbolizing that congregation for use on lapel pins, signs, letterheads, bumper stickers and caps, to honor traditions, to create a distinctive congregational song, to have a different set of robes for each choir, to insist on a formal installation service for the new minister, and to develop distinctive traditions for the celebration of certain holy occasions.

At this point some readers may ask, "Why not forget all that stuff and simply put our trust in the unity that we have in Jesus Christ as Lord and Savior?" There are at least three relevant responses to that question. First, throughout the Judeo-Christian tradition people have found it helpful to express their faith through the use of symbols, traditions, art, and distinctive customs. What is proposed here is nothing new. It is simply an affirmation of a centuries-old tradition. Second, the larger the collection of people, the more dependent those people are on symbolic expressions of unity. Historically, Christian communities that have banned symbols have (a) functioned as small rather than large congregations and (b) replaced physical symbols with a series of symbolic traditions and customs often including a distinctive form of dress. Third, throughout history sinful human beings have had to be reminded, often through symbolic acts and events, of God's presence in the world and of his love for his children. Symbols have always been important in expressing the faith.

The fourth reason that large congregations should reflect on the lessons to be found in the tribal analogy is that it can be used to explain and legitimatize differences among congregations. In many denominational families, for example, one system of church government is recommended or required for all congregations in that denomination. However, if one views the fellowship church as a family, the small church as a clan, the large church as a tribe, and the mini-denomination size church as a nation, the question is raised as to whether each should use the same form of congregational organization. Perhaps it is not just acceptable, but essential to adapt the form of church government to the nature of the institution as reflected in the size of the congregation.

The same point can be made when the discussion is shifted to the organization of the youth program, the role of the governing board, the responsibilities of the tribal chief, or the structure of the women's organization. Things are rarely the same in a family as in a tribe or a nation.

Finally, this analogy can be helpful in understanding the change in institutional context when a member leaves a clan to join a tribe or a minister leaves a tribe to join the staff of a nation. When such changes are perceived as simply moves from church A to church B, the complications that often accompany such a change are understated.

The more clearly leaders of larger churches recognize the similarities between a large congregation and the functioning of a tribe, the easier it will be for them to understand what is happening and to respond creatively to those tribal pressures.

What Are the Advantages?

The central thesis of this chapter is that those larger congregations that operate with a multiple staff are different from smaller churches.

Larger congregations tend to be more impersonal, to emphasize the functional aspects of the church rather than to undergird the relational dimensions of congregational life, to place greater demands on the staff in general and on the senior minister in particular, to have a higher proportion of relatively inactive members, to encounter more difficulty in recruiting and maintaining a network of lay volunteers, and to encourage a passive role among the laity. On a per member basis, the larger congregations also tend to be more expensive operations than are middle-sized or small churches.

At this point the reader may be asking, "If that's all true, why do we need large churches? Why don't we discourage the emergence of large churches and encourage the development of more middle-sized congregations?"

There are two basic reasons why that would be an unwise strategy. First, the large churches are where the people are found. In broad general terms, people appear to prefer larger churches. In the United Presbyterian Church, for example, the 50 largest congregations have a combined membership of approximately 150,000 communicants, about the same as the combined membership of the 2,500 smallest congregations. The 100 largest United Methodist congregations have a combined membership of 365,000, the same as the combined membership of the 8,500 smallest congregations in that denomination. The 750 largest United Methodist congregations report a combined total membership of 1.4 million members, the same total as the combined membership of the 18,000 smallest congregations in the denomination. In the Southern Baptist Convention the 2,500 largest congregations account for approximately 4 million members, the same as the combined membership of the 23,500 smallest SBC congregations. In other words, one basic reason for encouraging the existence of large congregations is that they are the simplest way of reaching large numbers of people with the Good News of Jesus Christ.

The second reason is that the larger churches, because of their size, concentration of resources, and unique characteristics often can provide a ministry to people who are largely ignored by the vast

44

majority of congregations. Examples of these specialized ministries include a ministry with single parents, a program for the developmentally disabled, a group for parents who recently experienced the death of a child, a ministry to alcoholics and their families, or an educational program for the visually handicapped. Very few of the traditionally family-oriented churches are able to serve these people.

In addition, large churches usually have the capability to provide a variety of ministries and programs for their members that is beyond the capability of four out of five congregations. These range from an array of adult study groups to a variety of choirs to a choice of three or four different worship experiences every weekend to exchange visits with churches on another continent to several "tracks" for the package of youth programs.

In other words, it appears that large churches, at least in part because of a larger program, can reach and serve more people in their efforts to proclaim the Gospel. Some of the price tags on that capability have been identified earlier, and it is important not to minimize this negative side of the balance sheet.

What Are the Points of Vulnerability?

The long established, stable small church is a tough, resilient, and tenacious religious institution. It is relatively immune to the shocks that often accompany a change of pastors. Small churches often are largely controlled by the laity, rather than by the clergy, and often one or two or three families exercise most of this control. Two or three families often are able to maintain a faltering small congregation and keep it from disappearing.

By contrast, larger churches are comparatively fragile and two or three families are less important in the overall support of the large church. Larger congregations usually are much more dependent on the paid staff. An unfortunate match in the ministerial placement process will be more destructive in larger churches. Short pastorates also tend to be more disruptive in larger churches. Destructive staff conflicts, which do not happen in small churches with only one minister on the payroll, can be very serious diversions from ministry in large churches.

Heavy dependence on the paid staff is only one of a series of unique characteristics of the large church that both illustrate its distinctive personality and increase its institutional vulnerability. Before moving to a discussion of the staffing of large churches, it may be helpful to review several other points of vulnerability of the large congregations.

1. The larger the membership of a congregation, the greater the probability that the members will have little in common with one another. The less the members have in common with one another, the more difficult it is to maintain a sense of unity.

2. The larger the church and the longer it has been in existence, the greater the tendency for permission-withholders (as contrasted to permission-givers) to dominate the decision-making procedures. This pattern often tends to drive the younger, newer, less experienced and more creative potential leaders out of the congregation or into a more passive role.

3. In the vast majority of large congregations it is very, very easy for the individual to become convinced that his views are not heard, that when absent he is not missed, and that his contributions of time, talent, and prayer are unimportant. One result of this is a conflict between the need for a systematic and time-consuming approach to pastoral care and the institutional demands on the time of the ministerial staff resulting from the size and complexity of the organization.

4. The large church is highly vulnerable to the financial squeeze produced by an extended inflationary era. This is especially important in the last third of the twentieth century which has produced the longest inflationary cycle in American history. While many church members do tithe, not all do, and an increasing proportion of those who do tithe do not give all of that tithe to the congregation in which they hold membership. People tend to give in response to their perception of need (note the impact of television on certain special appeals). In the large church it is more difficult for all (or at least most) of the members to be aware of the financial needs and obligations of

their church. Rarely are more than a handful of people adequately informed about the total ministry and program of the large congregation. One result is that most people are not fully aware of financial realities and increase their giving at the rate of only 2, 3, or 4 percent per year rather than the 6, 8, or 10 percent that is necessary to avoid cutbacks in program and outreach.

5. A fifth point of vulnerability in the large church that is related to financial problems is the tendency of the large congregation to suffer from an inadequate internal system of communication. A disproportionately large number of members are "out of touch" with the large congregation.

This is an especially serious problem in those denominations, such as the United Methodist Church and the Christian Church (Disciples of Christ) where the system of congregational self-government is based on giving a high priority to the goals of representation and participation. (This is in contrast to Presbyterian, Lutheran, and Episcopal systems which place a high priority on performance.) When the system of church government emphasizes participation and/or representation, this often leads to the assumption that members will know what is happening as a result of their participation. In fact, however, in very large congregations this usually means that 97 to 99 percent of the church members are not present for the monthly meeting of that congregation's governing body and therefore are not informed.

6. Larger churches tend to be especially vulnerable to discontent. The three most widely read indicators of the institutional health of a congregation are (a) increases or decreases in membership, (b) increases or decreases in the dollar receipts from member giving, and (c) face-to-face conversations. Each one has great value when used with smaller congregations. In larger churches, however, these three indicators often tend to conceal discontent rather than to recognize unhappiness.

One of the most widely used channels of communication for members to signal their discontent is to reduce their financial support. When this message is sent by five or six members of a large congregation, it does not carry the impact that it does when five or six members do the same in a small church. Furthermore, in large churches this message of unhappiness from a member may be largely concealed by the increased giving of newer members, by the impact of inflation, or by receipts from endowment funds and similar sources.

As a general rule, the larger the congregation the smaller the proportion of members who are present for worship on any given Sunday. Furthermore, larger churches tend to offer two, three, or four worship experiences on Sunday morning. As a result, the members who express their discontent by staying away from corporate worship often are not noticed but since their name remains on the membership roster their discontent is concealed.

Finally, the larger the congregation, the smaller the proportion of members who are involved in frequent face-to-face conversations with the staff and/or the lay leadership. Anonymity increases at the expense of intimate fellowship as a church grows in size. This increased anonymity can conceal discontent.

In summary larger churches tend to be especially vulnerable to discontent because it often reaches the boiling point before it is discovered. When discontent is discovered, it may be too late for a creative response or the size of the congregation, in proportion to the number of discontented members, may tempt leaders to conduct a Watergate-type of response to the unrest.

7. Perhaps the most serious point of institutional vulnerability in the large church is a direct result of its huge and unnatural size. One result of the huge size is that for the large church to remain on a plateau in size it must receive a great many new members every year. The typical 2000-member congregation, for example, must receive an average of three or four new members every week to replace those who move away, die, withdraw, or become inactive. That means a continuous influx of strangers to be assimilated. It is easier, more comfortable, and less disruptive for that 2000-member congregation to be content to receive only fifty new members annually and to gradually dwindle in size. The numerical decline can be rationalized by explaining, "But, we're still receiving more new

members every year than nine out of ten churches. What more can anyone expect of us?"

8. The large church also is vulnerable to the temptation to substitute a landlord role for ministry. The larger the congregation the greater the temptation to subordinate the active ministries of word and sacrament, Christian witness, evangelism and education to a lesser place in favor of the more passive role of housing social welfare programs sponsored by community agencies. This "busy-building" syndrome is a means of rationalizing what that congregation is not doing in creating new ministries to reach persons largely overlooked by other churches. Vulnerability to the landlord role is especially pronounced in those large congregations which draw most of their members from outside the neighborhood in which the meeting place is located. [8]

9. Many large congregations that have enjoyed a distinctive role in the past, and which include many longtime members in the leadership positions, are vulnerable to the normal institutional pressures to attempt to recreate yesterday in planning for tomorrow.

This same pressure also may be present in other types and sizes of congregations, but it often is more serious in large churches where congregations frequently have to make many changes to "keep up" with a changing world. By contrast, many smaller and more stable churches are more "apart" from the world and can perpetuate yesterday. Therefore, the pressures to recreate yesterday tend to be somewhere between irrelevant and destructive in larger churches that must adjust to a large passing parade of members, while these same pressures can be reassuring to many small churches where the church is a refuge of familiar people gathered together to escape from a changing world. Thus what is destructive in one may be institutionally reassuring in the other. In the middle-sized congregation the community context will be more influential in forcing members to recognize that tomorrow will be different. The huge congregation, however, often insulates itself from the community context and can function as a large, self-contained, and independent institution that is determined to perpetuate an increasingly obsolete pattern of performance in ministry.

These are a few of the points at which the large, and especially the long-established large congregation, is more vulnerable to institutional blight than are smaller and less complicated parishes. Institutional vulnerability also is part of the context in which the multiple staff functions in the large church; therefore, it is appropriate to shift the discussion from the institutional context of the multiple staff to the question of staffing the large church. An appropriate point for beginning that discussion is to look at the multiple staff picture in general and at a determination of staff needs in particular.

CHAPTER TWO
Staffing the Large Church

"What do you think of this proposal to add a third pastor to the staff?" asked John Ellis of his friend and fellow church member, Roger Erickson, as they drove to work together on Monday morning.

"I'm opposed to it myself," continued the 56-year-old Ellis. "My wife and I joined Bethel back in 1951 when Dr. Hanson was pastor. He retired in the early 1960s, and I can remember that somewhere around 1960 we peaked with over one thousand confirmed members. Hanson did it all by himself. Soon after we called his successor we added a second pastor.

"Now we're down to 800 members and people are talking about adding a third minister. We don't need that many chiefs."

"I agree with you, John," replied Erickson. "Last summer in Minnesota my wife and I visited a Lutheran parish that is slightly larger than Bethel and they have one pastor, a church secretary, and a custodian. But we have two ministers, two women in the office, and a full-time custodian for a congregation with a smaller membership. We already have a pretty big payroll for a middle-sized parish."

"I guess we might as well face it," sighed a member of the church council at the 625-member Grace Church. "We either watch the Sunday school and the youth program continue to decline or we go out and hire someone to build it up again. According to the pastor a parish as large as ours needs at least a part-time person who can specialize in youth and Christian education if we really want to be competitive in those areas. Maybe the time has come for Grace Church to add a second minister to the staff."

"That may be true, but I need more convincing," responded a longtime member. "Back in the 1950s we had a much bigger Sunday school and twice as many kids in the Luther League as we have now, and the pastor did it all by himself."

"Pastor, we've been friends for a long time now," declared Ken Richards as he settled into a comfortable chair in the office of the senior minister at First Church. "I know you are overworked and I think I can understand why you want to add a third minister to our staff, but what does Harry do? He's been the associate minister here for nearly two years, and, frankly, I don't know what he does with his time. I doubt if you're going to get much support for adding a third minister to the staff until the folks here are satisfied that we're getting our money's worth out of what we're paying Harry. Everybody likes him, but no one knows what he does."

"I can vote for expanding our program staff," reflected Marie Edwards. "If we want to grow, we need more staff, but why do we need so many people in the office? We have a business manager, a bookkeeper, a receptionist, three secretaries, and an administrative assistant to the senior minister. Couldn't we replace some of them with lay volunteers? Finally, I can't see why our director of Christian education needs a full-time secretary. Why can't we have a secretarial pool? Wouldn't that be less expensive?"

These comments raise a few of the questions that come up frequently when the discussion turns to staffing larger churches. One of the reasons why this topic raises so many questions is that the basic trend in American Protestantism is to increase the number of professional program staff members on the congregational roll.

Why More Staff?

There are at least eight reasons behind this basic trend. While not every reason applies to every congregation, it may be helpful to look at some of the reasons behind this increase in paid staff before shifting the discussion to more specific questions.

First, and perhaps most important, is the basic generalization that as an organization becomes more sensitive to the needs of individuals and to the differences among people, there is an increase in the complexity of that organization. Almost invariably this requires an increase in the number of staff persons in relationship to the number of persons served. This can be seen very clearly in religious organizations, medical services, banking, education, employer-employee relations, the military, environmental concerns, and many other person-centered organizations.

As a parish becomes more sensitive to the needs of people and to the differences among people, the program and ministry of that congregation becomes more complex. Thus the large, and especially the large and pluralistic parish, requires more staff than it needed back in 1955.

Closely related to this is the second factor, the increasing specialization of the American labor force. In 1930, for example, 17 percent of all physicians were specialists. Today that proportion has climbed to nearly 75 percent. The large church is no exception to this trend! Society is demanding specialists in health care, education, automobile mechanics, agriculture, athletics, and scores of other areas of life. An increasing number of parishes are seeking staff specialists in counseling, ministry to the elderly, education, evangelism, ministry with single adults, programs for the developmentally disabled, leadership development, administration, youth ministries, worship, ministry to single parents, community outreach, or some other program area. In general, the larger the membership the greater the demand for specialized staff.

Partly as a result of these two trends and partly as a reinforcement of them is a third factor. For the past three decades our society has been able to afford to encourage the emergence of differences among people. This can be seen with great visibility in men's clothing. More men's suits with the coat and trousers made of matching material were sold in 1932 than were manufactured four decades later. A more profound example of this trend can be seen in the modern high school which encourages differences among youth, which does not have a large core of courses that are required of everyone, which teaches youth that they cannot possibly say yes to every alternative in the curriculum and in extracurricular activities and that they should not feel guilty about saying no to most choices. This makes it very difficult for a parish to reach these same teenagers by offering a high school Sunday school class, only one youth group, perhaps a youth choir, and no alternatives for the traditional corporate worship experience on Sunday morning. This is but one part of a broad general increase in the pluralistic nature of our entire society. The more pluralistic the congregation, the greater the workload for staff.

A fourth factor is the gradual decline in the proportion of the population in a household composed of a husband and wife living together with children under eighteen at home and the wife not employed outside the home. This has been the traditional "target population" of the thousands of "family-oriented" congregations. Among other positive values, wives provided a large core of lay volunteers for the typical family-oriented parish. In 1979, however, less than 10 percent of all families fit into that category. There are almost as many one-parent families in the nation as there are families in which the husband and wife are both present; there are also children under eighteen living in homes where the wife is not employed outside the home! This means a more sensitive and complex ministry is required of the parish to reach a more varied range of households. Between 1950 and 1975 the number of employed men in the civilian labor force increased by 22 percent, the number of working women increased by 14 percent, but the number of married working women, living with their husband and with children under eighteen at home increased by 217 percent from 3.6 million to 11.4 million.

This means an increase in complexity and a decrease in the number of women who are available as lay volunteers in the typical parish. One response is to replace lay volunteers with paid staff.

A fifth factor behind the increase in the number of paid professional staff members is the general drift in our society toward "hiring someone else to do it." This can be seen in the decrease in home auto repairs, the increase in the number of babysitters, the decrease in the proportion of people preparing their own income tax returns, and the increased expectations placed on the paid staff members of the parish.

A sixth factor has been the "Americanization" of many congregations which were founded as nationality or language parishes. This change has produced a demand for more staff. When the members of a congregation feel a sense of unity and cohesiveness because of a common nationality background, regardless of whether it be German, Danish, Dutch, Swedish, Italian, Norwegian, Welsh, Finnish, Korean, Latvian, or Japanese, this "glue" enables that congregation to function with fewer professional staff members than is required in the same size parish where that nationality or language "glue" has disappeared. This trend can be seen very clearly in hundreds of Lutheran parishes and is beginning to appear in the Reformed Church in America, the Christian Reformed Church, and the Mennonite Churches.

A seventh factor is that in today's American society the loyalty of individuals to institutions is not being passed on by inheritance as it was a generation ago. Institutions are less likely to inherit the loyalty of younger people than formerly was the pattern. Institutions must re-earn the loyalty of each new generation. This can be seen in private colleges, service clubs, labor unions, fraternal organizations and lodges, Scouting and the churches. To re-earn the loyalty of a new generation often requires a larger staff.[1]

An eighth reason for the increase in paid staff is a result of the fact that the number of persons marrying across denominational lines is increasing. When a Lutheran married a Lutheran or a Presbyterian married a Presbyterian, it was much easier for the spouse to be assimilated into a new congregation. As more people "marry into" a congregation from outside that denominational family, the load on the professional staff increases. This can be seen most clearly in the Episcopal Church and the Christian Church (Disciples of Christ), but is beginning to be more visible in Lutheran, Methodist, and Baptist congregations where marriage across denominational lines was much less common in the 1950s than it is today.

One of the many factors behind this increase in the number of persons marrying across denominational lines is that a smaller proportion of young people are going to church-related colleges. While it was rarely mentioned openly, one of the reasons for the church-related college was to increase the probability that a Lutheran coed would meet and marry a Lutheran young man or that a Presbyterian would meet and eventually marry a Presbyterian. In 1950, for example, slightly less than one-half of all persons enrolled in colleges and universities attended private institutions and slightly over one-half attended public colleges. By 1979 the proportion attending private schools had dropped to less than one-fourth and a larger proportion of young adults are meeting their future spouse on the campus of a public college.

The smaller the proportion of members who were reared within that denominational tradition, the larger the workload for paid staff members.

While this is not offered as a complete list, these eight factors have been significant forces behind the increase in paid staff in the larger congregations of nearly every denominational family. From this general background, it may be appropriate next to raise two very specific policy questions that should be asked in each large congregation that is debating the issue of the size of the program staff.

Growth, Plateau or Decline?

The majority of all congregations averaging more than 200 at worship on Sunday morning are staffed either to remain on a plateau or to decline in size. Only a small proportion are staffed for numerical growth. This is a simple descriptive statement based on first-hand contact with hundreds of large churches. It is not a statement of values. Such values are determined by congregational leaders.

Perhaps the most widespread example of this descriptive statement is the congregation averaging 200, 250, or 300 at worship and who finds it needs to undertake an extensive construction program to house its program. A very common pattern has been to finance a part of the cost of that construction project by not employing additional program staff. This "savings" in salaries is used to help meet the interest and principal payments on the mortgage. A common result of that procedure is the construction of attractive new rooms that are either empty or only partially filled because the program was not built to fill those rooms.

A second pattern is for a congregation to double in size under the leadership of an extraordinarily talented minister with a magnetic personality, but not to add the program staff persons necessary to help in the assimilation of the large influx of new members. When that remarkably gifted minister moves on and is replaced by an ordinary human being, that growth begins to melt away and the congregation moves back toward its former size.

In both of these examples the decision not to expand the program staff represents an inconsistency between a basic goal of the congregation—to register numerical growth—and the value system of the leadership—not to increase the amount paid for staff salaries. This inconsistency between goals and values is a very sure method of producing frustration over results.

While there is no evidence to prove that either long pastorates or expansion of the program staff will produce numerical growth in a church, there is very persuasive evidence that suggests it is rare to find a growing congregation *that has sustained its growth over a long period of time* that has not had the benefits of both long pastorates and an adequate program staff.

In simple terms, perhaps the first question the leaders of a large congregation should consider as they look at the ratio of program staff to the size of that congregation is, "Are we staffing for numerical growth, for remaining on a plateau, or for eventual decline?" The answer to that question can be used to test the consistency between goals and values.

Is your congregation staffed to grow, decline, or remain on a plateau?

What Is Not Getting Done?

The second of the two basic policy questions concerns the discussion of the duties and responsibilities of the program staff. The usual response when someone proposes adding a new staff position to the budget of a congregation is to ask, "What will that person do?" This is a logical and rational question, but it is diversionary. A much better question is to ask, "What is not getting done now, because we are understaffed, that will tend to undercut the life and program of this congregation, but whose consequences will not be felt for another five or six years?"

An example of such delayed consequences can be found in the opening paragraphs of this chapter. Bethel Church, under the leadership of Dr. Hanson, apparently was understaffed back in the 1950s. The congregation found it easier to receive new members than to assimilate them into the fellowship of the parish. When his twenty-year pastorate came to an end in the early 1960s, a major ingredient in the "glue" that held that congregation together disappeared—as did a couple of hundred members. The consequences of not adding a second pastor back in the 1950s were not felt until after Dr. Hanson retired. What did not happen in the assimilation of new members, in the expansion of the program, and in the development of a larger leadership core was not felt until several years later.

In general terms there are four important responsibilities that often are neglected in large understaffed churches. One of these, the failure to assimilate new members into the fellowship of the church, is very common in large churches. A second is the lack of a consistent leadership development program to provide a continuing supply of competent and self-confident lay volunteers to replace the persons who move away or retire and to staff new ministries. A third deficit frequently produced by understaffing is in program. Many large

58

congregations have too few classes, choirs, study groups, prayer cells, circles in the women's organization, youth fellowships, outreach programs, and mission groups for the number of members. One result of underprogramming is an excessively large proportion of relatively inactive members. A fourth result of understaffing in many large churches is a deterioration of the new member recruitment system because of staff neglect. When this phase of congregational life is understaffed, it is the equivalent of a decision to staff for a decline in the size of that congregation. What is not getting done in your church because it is understaffed?

How Many Staff Members Are Needed?

A third basic generalization that forms part of the context, or frame of reference, when looking at staff needs is the ratio of staff to the size of a parish.

In chapter 1 it was pointed out that there are great variations among congregations in how they "count" members. Therefore a more useful statistical index for measuring the size of a congregation is the average attendance at worship on Sunday morning.

As a *beginning* point in looking at the number of paid professional staff, the table below shows the ratio in the typical mainline Protestant congregation. Remember, this is only a *beginning* point. In general, there are *fewer* full-time program staff positions than shown here in congregations which display several of the following characteristics: (a) it is less than 15 years old, (b) the members are paying off a large mortgage or in a major building program, (c) it is composed largely of young

Professional Staff Positions	
Average Attendance at Worship	Full-Time Program Staff Positions
200	1
300	2
400	3
500	4
600	5
700	6
800	7
900	7 or 8

families living in two-generation house-holds, (d) the members share the same very strong nationality, ethnic, or language tie, (e) the pastor has been serving that same congregation for at least a dozen years, (f) most of the members are located at the conservative end of the theological spectrum, (g) the church is growing very rapidly, (h) it is built around the personality of the pastor, (i) the members either live in the same geographical community and/or come from the same social-economic educational-theological background, (j) the annual death rate is less than 0.7 per 100 members, (k) the membership includes a large proportion of extroverted "joiners" who have an unusually high level of competence in building relationships with strangers, (l) the adult members are drawn largely from the 25–55 age bracket, (m) the organizational life functions around the intentional use of large groups and there is a limited emphasis on small groups, (n) the program staff members have a long tenure on the staff of that congregation, and/or (o) the congregation is affiliated with the American Lutheran Church, the Lutheran Church-Missouri Synod, the North American Baptist Conference, the Baptist General Conference, or the Christian Reformed Church.

On the other hand, many congregations have a *larger* number of full-time program staff positions than is reflected in this table. In general, these congregations display several of the following characteristics: (a) it is more than 80 years old, (b) the church once averaged more than 300 at worship on Sunday morning but has been declining in size, (c) it serves a heterogeneous, pluralistic, and diverse membership, (d) a large proportion of members were not reared in that denominational family, (e) the annual death rate is above 2 per 100 members, (f) the membership is widely scattered, (g) the senior pastor has been serving this congregation for less than seven years, (h) there is no major indebtedness, (i) the congregation has emphasized a strong service or Christian witness ministry to residents of the neighborhood in which the meeting place is located, (j) less than 30 percent of adult members (age 18 and over) live in households consisting of husband and wife with children under 18 at home, (k) more than 12 percent of adult members are widowed but not remarried, (l) the median age of adult members (age 18 and over) is 50 or higher, (m) the membership roster includes a large number of dependent personalities and/or shy and bashful individuals, (n) there is strong emphasis on small groups in the organizational life of the parish, (o) there is an average of 65 or more households per 100 members, (p) the members display a broad-based support for the goal of reversing the recent decline in membership, attendance, and participation, and/or (q) the congregation is affiliated with the Episcopal Church or the Christian Church (Disciples of Christ).

The music staff (choir director, organists, music directors, *et al.*) should NOT be included in these calculations on staff size unless (a) there is major emphasis on a large number of choirs as part of the group life of that parish, and (b) there is at least one full-time person specializing in music.

In looking at the table it is important to note that it reflects *positions*, not staff members. It is not uncommon for a congregation to fill what once was a full-time position for one person with two, three, or four part-time specialists. For example, a 135-year-old congregation that averages 400 at worship and recently began to pursue an aggressive evangelistic strategy has developed a program staff that includes a full-time senior minister, a full-time associate minister who serves as program director, a one-third time lay woman responsible for staffing the new-member recruitment campaign, a one-third time lay woman in leadership development, a one-third time youth director, a half-time person in Christian education, in addition to four part-time specialists in the music program. (The combined salaries of these four part-time staff persons in music is somewhat less than one-half the compensation package granted the associate minister.)

Ordained or Lay?

A fourth and very significant part of the context when looking at program staff is illustrated in this example. This is the trend away from the traditional emphasis on full-time ordained ministers and toward a larger number of lay staff members, many of whom are part-time. The biggest change has been the employment of more lay women in program staff positions. It is not unusual, for example, to find a parish which formerly had three full-time ordained clergy on the staff now to be staffed with two clergy and to have filled the third position with two or three lay women with combined salaries totalling less than the amount that had been required for the salary, housing allowance, and pension of an ordained minister. In one such case the congregation decided to replace a minister who had resigned with three part-time lay women. One was paid $8,000 a year to be responsible for member-oriented program development, another was paid $5,000 as a half-time community worker, and the third received $4,000 annually to provide staff assistance to the evangelism committee in its visitation evangelism efforts and to be responsible for the assimilation of each of the recent new adult members.

Thousands of lay women are serving today as directors or teachers in church-sponsored weekday nursery schools, as assistants to the pastor, as program coordinators, as leadership development specialists, as youth directors, as church business administrators, as community workers, as educational assistants, as parish visitors, as recreation center directors, as directors of the parish communication's network, or as specialists in a single area of program such as a ministry with single adults or with the recently widowed. The typical lay woman on a parish program staff often is in the 35 to 60 age bracket, married (it appears an increasing proportion are widowed, separated, or divorced), but the youngest child is old enough that she is not required to be at home all day; she does not need or does not want a full-time job, she wants some control over her hours; she has a deep commitment to both Christ as Lord and Savior and to the church; she enjoys church work; she has been blessed with gifts of creativity, organizational skills, and/or the ability to relate to the shy, the timid, and the introverted; she seeks a chance to express her gifts through the church; she finds fulfillment in this role; and she probably has had little or no formal training for the particular staff position she now holds, except for brief workshops and institutes she has attended since being employed in this role. Perhaps one-third were not members of the congregation now employing them when first hired. Many are exteachers. A substantial number never had been employed outside the home before, and many began their career as a church secretary. Some are employed on a full-time basis, but most receive less than a full-time salary.

While it would be unrealistic to suggest that women are the only lay persons being employed as program staff members, there are several reasons why this trend is in the direction of an increasing number of women on the program staff. The most influential factor is that while the marketplace has provided many employment opportunities for talented men, far fewer opportunities have been available to women born before 1940. Despite the recent rapid increase in the employment of women outside the home, women still constitute the only large reservoir of talented but unemployed adults in the total population. A second reason is that few men are interested in part-time employment while many women do not want full-time jobs. A third reason is that frequently women can be employed to do the same work for a lower salary than would be paid a man. This difference is especially pronounced between the lay woman and the ordained man. While this is unfair, it is a fact of life and an important reason for the shift to more women staff members. Although it is seldom discussed openly, a fourth reason is that many congregations will look for two or three part-time women staff members to fill the vacancy created by the departure of an ordained staff member because they know they will have fewer problems in terminating the employment of a part-time lay woman than in getting rid of an ordained minister. Fifth, it often is easier to find a gifted lay woman to fill a staff position than it is to find an ordained and equally talented man who is willing to accept the second, third, or fourth place in the parish pecking order. Finally, as a group mature women generally have more skill and considerably more practice in "getting along" with men than do most male members of the adult male population.

This last point was illustrated when a Lutheran parish in Pennsylvania replaced the departing associate minister with a lay woman. Subsequently, she was asked, "How do you expect to be able to get along with a senior pastor who has gone through five associates in eight years? Why do you think you will be able to stick in there when none of those five men was able to last more than two years?" "Two reasons," she replied simply. "First, I am not ordained. Second, I'm a woman. I won't be a threat to him." As the number of women ministers holding the office of senior minister begins to rise, as it will during the latter part of the 1980s, a new dynamic will be introduced into this subject of lay staff members, but it is too early to predict the consequences of that change.

Members or Non-Members?

"All right, suppose we do decide to include part-time or full-time laypersons on our program staff, should we hire members or nonmembers?" This is one of the most frequently raised questions as a congregation builds its staff. The question does not have a simple and universal answer that applies to all situations. There are advantages and disadvantages on either side of the issue. Seeking a member to fill a program staff position usually means that the new employee will be familiar with the distinctive personality of the church and its members, with the strengths and weaknesses of the minister(s), with denominational jargon and polity, and with the customs and traditions of the congregation.

The obvious disadvantages of employing a member include the objection, "Why are we paying her when the rest of us volunteer our time and talent?" the occasionally very traumatic experience of terminating an employment arrangement with a member who is not interested in resigning, the question of potential conflict of interests when an employee (or the employee's spouse) holds a very influential policy-making office, the possible embarrassment created when an exemployee now holds an influential policy-making office, the danger of excessive gossip about office events or staff relationships, the unrealistic expectations often placed on a member who is a paid program staff member to also contribute a large amount of volunteer time, the tendency to fail to express an appropriate degree of appreciation to the program staffer who also is a member because her efforts tend to be taken for granted, and the reluctance in many congregations to finance continuing education experiences for a member who is on the staff when that "fringe benefit" is not available to lay volunteers. Another potential disadvantage of employing members is represented by the comment, "When we hired Sally to be a full-time educational assistant, we gained a tremendous person for our staff, but we also lost the services of the best lay volunteer this congregation has ever had."

From this observer's experiences it appears that the disadvantages of employing a member and the advantages of hiring a nonmember outweigh the other side of the equation by a 65–35 ratio.

This raises two additional questions. How do we find a nonmember to add to our program staff? What are the advantages of employing a nonmember? Responses to both of these questions can be found in the experiences of one congregation.

"After the Session authorized the position of a program coordinator on a half-time basis," explained the senior minister at Knox Presbyterian Church, "I went over to visit each of the other three senior ministers of large churches around here. I described the type of position we were trying to fill, the kind of person we were looking for, and the amount of money we had available. Chuck Peterson, over at Trinity Lutheran Church, told me that he knew exactly the person we were looking for. He introduced me to a fifty-one year old woman in his parish who had been widowed two years earlier. She had taught school for five or six years before and immediately after she had been married, but had not been employed outside the home for more than twenty years. When I met her, she had begun to think about getting a job. Her husband had provided for her through life insurance, a paid-for home, and some savings, but inflation was eating into what once would have been seen as a very comfortable income. Their youngest child was a junior in high school at the time. We agreed that the average work week for a professional in the church is approximately fifty hours, and so we pay her a half-time salary for twenty-five hours a week. She actually puts in at least thirty hours, but she insists on half-time salary because she has considerable control over when she works."

"What do you get for that half-time salary?" was the next question asked of the senior minister at Knox Church.

"Well, she's been with us for six years now, so I believe I can answer that," he replied. "First of all, we got the program coordinator we were looking for. Actually she really is both program developer and program coordinator. In the six years she has been with us, we have doubled the number of small and middle-size groups that meet on a regular basis and more than doubled the number of participants. For example, she has a cousin who is a missionary in South America, so she organized a mission study group of about a dozen people that spent a week in Guyana with this Lutheran missionary. They came back and have given our emphasis on missions a tremendous shot in the arm. Next year she has arranged to take a group to visit a Presbyterian mission in Brazil. In other words, we got a very creative and energetic person with lots of imagination, initiative, and drive. In that respect our expectations have been more than fulfilled. In addition, although we didn't even know we needed this when we created the position, we have added a staff member who brings a different perspective, a different set of experiences, and a different understanding of church polity to Knox Church. One of her major contributions is in the questions she raises about why we do that or why we don't do this. Having a Lutheran on our staff has certainly broadened my perspective and caused me to rethink some of the traditions and customs I had always accepted without question."

"Where is she on Sunday morning? Here or in her own church?" was the next question asked of the Presbyterian pastor.

"To some extent the answer to that question is yes," replied the obviously very pleased senior minister. "Her church offers an 8:00 A.M. worship service and she usually attends that and comes over here about 9:15. Our schedule begins with worship at 8:30 followed by church school at 9:45 and worship at 11:00, so she is here for most of the morning, but she insists that not be counted as part of her twenty-five hours a week. She worships with us at 11 o'clock about half the time, but she often is involved in some special programs planned for the people who come to the early service and thus have the time for two or two and a half hour programs following the close of the first worship service.

"Now, let me answer three questions you didn't ask," concluded the senior minister. "First, we have no one griping about paying a member for what should be done by a lay volunteer. No one would expect a Lutheran lay woman to come over and be a volunteer in a Presbyterian church. Second, if and when the time should come that my successor would want to terminate her employment, he won't be faced with the problem of firing a member. Third, contrary to what some of us feared, Chuck Peterson is not mad at us for stealing one of his lay volunteers. He is proud of what has happened. He and I both believe that one of the purposes of the church is to enable persons to blossom forth and to become the kind of person the Creator intended. This has happened with this woman. In addition, Chuck says that because of her experiences here at Knox, she is a more self-confident, creative, and valuable lay volunteer at Trinity than she was before we hired her. This has turned out to be one of those ideas that produced at least three winners—Knox Presbyterian, Trinity Lutheran, and the lady we hired!"

Part-Time or Full-Time?

While it overlaps the previous discussions on lay or ordained staff and on choosing a member or a nonmember, there is still another dimension of this subject that should be explored. This is the policy question of concentrating on full-time persons in developing a multiple staff or on encouraging the employment of part-time persons.

There are at least a half dozen considerations that should be taken into account in reflecting on this policy issue.

Perhaps the first, and certainly one of the most important of these factors, is the leadership style of the senior minister. If the senior minister is most comfortable supervising staff members by spending considerable time with each member on a one-to-one basis, it probably would be inadvisable to encourage the employment of part-time program staff persons. If, however, the senior minister is comfortable delegating responsibilities to staff and does not feel the need for large amounts of one-to-one time with each member of the staff, there are many advantages to the use of part-time staff.

Many senior ministers find it much easier to supervise the part-time specialist, who carries only two or three precisely defined responsibilities, than to oversee the work of a generalist who carries a variety of changing responsibilities. Others are more comfortable with a smaller staff composed largely of full-time generalists, each of whom can carry out several assignments. This means that the leadership style and the preferences of the senior minister should be the first factor to be considered in choosing between a concentration of part-time or full-time staff members. This is also another of a long list of reasons why large congregations should encourage long tenure for the senior minister.

A second variable is the size of the staff. When the professional program staff includes more than seven persons, it begins to be difficult to plan and conduct creative and productive staff meetings with a sense of full participation by all persons present. A program staff meeting including two or three full-time members and three or four part-time persons can be a very productive experience. It is far more difficult to have an equally productive staff meeting when the participants include four or five full-time ministers and six or seven part-time lay program-staff members. The full-time ministers often unintentionally dominate the meeting and cause the part-time persons to feel they are of marginal importance. This is partly a result of the "professionalism" of the ministers, partly a result of the size of the group, partly a natural product of the fact that the full-time persons often feel they have a greater stake in what is happening than do part-time persons, and partly a product of the deference pyramid which places (a) ordained persons and (b) full-time employees above part-time lay persons in the pecking order.

A third variable that should be considered in choosing between part-time and full-time persons on the professional staff is the matter of supply and demand. In general, our society still expects most persons in the labor force to be employed on a full-time basis. The number of persons interested in and available for part-time employment is rising more rapidly than is the number of part-time jobs. This is especially true for professionals. Therefore, most large churches will be able to choose from among a larger number of candidates if the post to be filled is a part-time position than if the search is for a full-time staff member. One example was mentioned earlier of the part-time lay woman who neither wants nor needs a full-time job. Another is the underemployed pastor of the small rural church (or two-church parish) who serves as the part-time associate minister of the church in town that needs additional program staff, but cannot afford a second (or third) minister on a full-time basis. A third example is the high school social science teacher who is the part-time youth director for a large church. A fourth example of this pattern is the ordained minister who has a 40 or 44 hour per week position with a social welfare agency and serves on the staff of a large congregation on a part-time basis to help with the peak hour load on weekends and/or to staff a specialized program such as a ministry with single adults. A fifth example of the availability of part-time staff is the public school teacher or administrator who has specialized in the education of handicapped children and is employed on a part-time basis to help a congregation develop a large scale summer program for handicapped children. In general, it is easier to find part-time workers, and especially part-time persons with highly specialized skills, than it is to find full-time staff members.

A fourth, and somewhat more subjective factor is productivity. In general, the church with part-time professional staff members receives more "bang for the buck," in terms of productivity, from its part-time program staff than does the church with full-time generalists.

A fifth and very subjective variable must be viewed in terms of interpersonal relationships. Every member of the large congregation does not enjoy an ideal interpersonal relationship with every member of the program staff. Some members of the program staff have a better relationship with Mr. Rizzo or Mrs. Newman than do other members of the staff. Therefore, the larger the staff, the greater the probability that Mr. Rizzo or Mrs. Newman will find someone on the staff who relates to him or to her on a satisfactory basis.

This is especially important in those program areas that are influenced by both relational and functional considerations. The most common example of this is the music program. In several large churches, for example, some members of the choir participate, despite their personal dislike for the choir director, because he is a superb director. Other potential members of the choir stay away because they do not like the choir director. In other large churches the pattern of participation is reversed when a less talented director enlists some members because of her winsome personality and her loving concern for people, but some potential choir members, who place a higher value on competence than on the director's personality, choose not to be members of the choir. (There is one large church in Texas where this is not a problem. The choir director is both a superb director and an exceptionally warm and attractive personality.) The large congregations that place a premium on *both* excellent vocal music *and* on a large number of choirs with broad participation from all age brackets usually achieve their goal only by employing several part-time choir directors. Some people relate to one director while others are more comfortable with another personality or style of directing.

The issue of interpersonal relationships is also important in staffing youth ministries, educational programs, visitation efforts, and new member recruitment strategies.

Finally, there is a point that often is overlooked in recruiting program staff. This is termination. Often it is easier to terminate the employment of a part-time staff person who is not completely economically dependent on that job, than it is to dismiss a full-time employee who is the principal breadwinner for a family or to discharge an ordained minister who often cannot leave until a new ministerial position has been secured. After having experienced the trauma of seeking to dismiss a full-time ordained staff member, several congregations have developed a strong preference for the part-time lay staff member!

It should be emphasized that not all congregations will give the same weight to each of these five variables in choosing between part-time or full-time program staff members.

Generalists or Specialists?

Another basic policy question in building a program staff overlaps the previous three sections of this chapter and concerns the distinction between generalists and specialists. Again, there is no one "right" answer that applies to every multiple staff. There are, however, five factors that should be considered in choosing a direction on this issue.

The first, and the most important, is the size of the congregation. In general, the larger the membership, and therefore the larger the program staff, the greater the need for specialists. The congregation averaging 300 at worship on Sunday morning may function effectively with two full-time ordained ministers and no other program staff, except for part-time persons in music. Both ministers are primarily generalists and share the work load.

By contrast, the congregation averaging 600 at worship may include on the program staff a senior minister, an associate pastor, a full-time specialist in Christian education, and four to six part-time specialists. One may specialize in youth ministries, another in leadership development, a third in visitation of shut-ins and the elderly, a fourth in the recruitment and assimilation of new members and a fifth in a special ministry with the elderly, single adults, families that include a handicapped member, or in some form of community outreach. In many of these congregations the full-time associate minister is a generalist who also specializes as program director. In addition, that congregation may employ two, three, or four specialists to staff the several components of the music program.

71

The second variable in choosing between generalists and specialists is the often neglected factor of satisfaction and motivation. Today in any organization every person needs independently verifiable measurements for gaining the satisfaction of knowing "I'm doing a good job in what I'm expected to do here." The larger and/or the more complex the organization, the more relevant that generalization. The specialist, who by definition usually has a reasonably clearly defined role, is more likely to secure those satisfactions more or less automatically than is the generalist who has a less clearly defined role.

In other words, the greater the tendency toward employing generalists on the program staff, the greater the need to build in satisfactions for those staff members.

The third factor goes back to the subject of supervision. In general, because of clarity of role definition and the built-in satisfactions that usually accompany a clearly defined role, it is easier for most senior ministers to supervise a staff composed largely of specialists than it is to supervise a staff of generalists. This does not apply to all senior ministers and certainly does not apply to those with both considerable skill and long experience in supervising a large program staff. Many senior ministers, however, who have little training and limited experience in supervising other professionals usually will find it easier to supervise specialists rather than generalists.

Closely related to this is a widely neglected fourth variable that deserves more attention. This is the "behavior setting," or the "deference pyramid," that influences the behavior of every staff member. One facet of this is seniority and tenure. Another is the distinction between the relational and functional aspects of ministry. The older staff member who is a generalist, who has been on the staff for many years, and who has built deep relationships with many members covering a broad range of concerns often is perceived as a threat by the recently arrived, younger senior minister. By contrast, the older staff member who is a specialist and who has been on the staff for many years usually is not perceived as a threat by the same newly arrived young senior minister.

72

There are four dimensions of this variable that deserve consideration here. First, the older person usually is higher on the deference pyramid or in the pecking order than the younger person. Second, the greater the seniority or the longer the tenure, the higher the place on the deference pyramid. Third, the person involved in the relational dimensions of ministry usually is higher on the deference pyramid than is the person responsible for clearly defined functions. Fourth, the generalist usually emphasizes relationships while the specialist often emphasizes functions. What does all of that add up to for this discussion? Frequently it means (a) the recently arrived senior minister often will feel more comfortable if the continuing staff is composed largely of specialists, and (b) the recently arrived senior minister often will feel a need to replace longtime staff members who clearly "outrank" him on the deference pyramid. In other words, the specialists are more likely to be asked to stay, and the generalists are more likely to be expected to leave when a new person assumes the office of senior minister.

Finally, this discussion on specialists or generalists on the program staff also goes back to the marketplace and the availability of potential new staff members. It appears that for the 1980s at least, the supply of part-time specialists will be greater than the supply of full-time generalists. In addition to being easier to recruit and to supervise, the part-time specialist, as contrasted with the full-time generalist, frequently finds it easier to fit into and fill a specific need on the program staff of the large congregation.

Should We Employ an Intern?

During the 1960s many Protestant seminaries moved from a standard three-year course of study to a four-year sequence that included a one-year internship for each seminarian. This, of course, has long been the practice in several Lutheran seminaries.

One result of this trend has been a sharp increase in the number of interns or vicars on the staffs of larger congregations. For some churches this was a transitional step between an era of only one pastor on the staff to a staff with two ordained ministers.

There are many excellent reasons for continuing the required year of internship for seminary students. It provides a year of para-professional experience. It offers an experience that is an important part of the context for that last year of seminary classes. It is a break in the academic routine. It enables the student to reflect on his or her call to the pastoral ministry in the context of parish life before making a major bilateral career decision. Perhaps most important of all, it provides for male seminarians (and eventually for female seminarians) a variety of role models of the parish pastor. A disproportionately large number of interns and vicars serve that year on the staff of multiple staff congregations. While the larger congregation with a multiple staff is not representative of a cross section of the churches seeking recent seminary graduates, it often provides a valuable year for the seminary student.

Too often, however, the seminary student is viewed by parishioners as the equivalent of a full-time staff member. Usually that is a deceptive concept and often produces an understaffed situation.

A more realistic approach would identify the stipend paid the intern as a legitimate benevolence expenditure by that parish for the training of future pastors rather than as a part of "staff salaries." (In some situations this point is reinforced by the fact that the intern's stipend is identified as a tax-free scholarship rather than as a taxable income.) Second, the intern needs and deserves considerable instruction and supervision by the senior pastor. Many of the classes, visits, programs, and events the intern participates in are part of the work of the senior minister or another permanent staff member; therefore, if the church gains as much in productivity in ministry as is required from the staff in a teaching and supervisory role, that should be considered a fair exchange. The purpose of the internship is to provide a year of experiential learning for the seminary student, not to supply cheap help for the parish! A third factor that often is overlooked is that most interns come into a strange situation and must develop a set of relationships with people before they can be effective contributors in

74

their ministry. A frequent complaint is, "Just when our vicar got to be really helpful, he finished his term here and went back to school." It is unreasonable to expect an inexperienced intern who will leave after nine to fifteen months, and when everyone knows the internship is a temporary arrangement, to be an effective full-time staff member in a large and complex parish.

Many large congregations can both afford and offer an excellent learning setting for an intern or vicar. They should be encouraged to include a position for an intern on the staff as a part of the continuing benevolence efforts of that parish. This can be communicated to the members by listing the stipend paid the intern under benevolences rather than under staff salaries. Occasionally they will benefit from an exceptionally talented intern who contributes far more than he or she receives in compensation and supervision. If that is regarded as an exception, rather than as the expected norm, everyone will be happier.

Many other large congregations, however, and especially those seeking to move from a status of being understaffed to an adequate level of staff, are tempted to see the use of an intern as a simple and low cost means of expanding the program staff. Frequently this is counterproductive. Many of the parishes seeking to reach a level of adequate program staffing cannot afford (a) the financial cost of an intern and/or (b) the periodic disruption created by the annual turnover of persons occupying that slot in the table of organization. On a cost-benefit basis they would be better off seeking permanent program staff rather than attempting to "get by" with a series of interns. One of the many reasons for this statement is that the understaffed church rarely can offer adequate supervision and instruction for the intern. If the senior minister does provide the supervision and care the intern has a right to expect, the usual result is that the effects of understaffing become even more apparent.

Fortunately, or unfortunately, there are enough self-motivated, exceptionally capable, completely committed, remarkably gifted, and highly personal interns and vicars coming out of the seminaries every year to tempt many leaders in understaffed churches to conclude, "If

75

we can find an intern of the quality that St. Mark's has, that will solve our staff needs and won't cost us much money."

Why Can't We Use More Volunteers?

After reading this far about several of the issues involved in building a program staff, some of the leaders from large congregations will be tempted to ask, "Why do we have to depend so much on paid staff? Why can't we make greater use of volunteers and cut down on paid staff? Smaller churches depend largely or sometimes exclusively on volunteers. Why can't we? Why do we have to go to the trouble and expense of building a large and expensive staff?

The heart of the response to those and similar questions is the theme of this book. *The very large congregation is not simply an enlarged version of the small church. The very large congregation is different!* (See pages 17-27.)

One of the important differences between small or middle-sized churches and the very large congregations is the development and maintenance of a network of volunteers. In the typical church the network of lay volunteers is reinforced by the fact that the members know one another personally and often many are related by blood or marriage. The work of volunteers is more likely to be recognized and appreciated. In larger congregations, self-imposed expectations in terms of quality of performance often are higher. Frequently the tasks are more difficult because of a greater emphasis on specialized ministries. The problems of internal communication and coordination are also greater in the very large congregation. In most cases the sheer size of a particular job increases with an increase in the size of the congregation. This can be illustrated by such offices as church treasurer, Sunday school superintendent, financial secretary, youth counselor, director of lay leadership development, president of the women's organization, director of the vacation Bible school, or custodian. All of these can be, and usually are filled by volunteers in thousands of small churches. Many of them require fifty to two hundred hours a year of volunteer effort. In the very large congregation, however, the person holding any one of these same offices may have to spend six hundred to over two thousand hours a year on that responsibility.

One response to that has been the widely used procedure of assigning a responsibility that requires perhaps one hundred hours a year in the small church, and is carried by one lay volunteer, to a dozen volunteers in the very large congregation with the expectation that each will contribute sixty to eighty hours of volunteer time. The usual results of that system include confusion, problems of coordination, an uneven quality of performance, and some unfulfilled expectations. The span of control is too broad for anyone to manage.

In other words, the dependence on paid staff in the very large congregations is not a luxury. It is basically a product of the distinctive characteristics of that size church.

What About the Pastor's Secretary?

In scores of very large congregations one of the two or three most valuable players on the staff team, and too often one of the least appreciated, is the senior pastor's secretary. In perhaps 98 percent of the churches this position is held by a woman so the female pronoun will be used in offering several generalizations.

Perhaps the most important, but seldom publicly recognized, characteristic of the senior minister's secretary is that her primary loyalty is to the senior minister, *not to the congregation that pays her salary!* The basic reason for this is the same as that of the President of the United States who usually feels it is necessary to choose as the undersecretary of each cabinet officer a person whose primary loyalty is to the President, not to that cabinet secretary nor to that department. The President needs a responsible person in each cabinet department who holds a primary loyalty to the President and who will not only not undercut the President's policies, but who also will attempt to make sure the department's actions will be compatible with the President's goals. Franklin D. Roosevelt and John F. Kennedy both followed that principle, while Jimmy Carter encouraged most of the cabinet officers to

77

pick their own staff members and thus created many difficulties for himself.

From this observer's perspective the best secretaries for senior pastors have a strong primary loyalty to the senior minister. That means they do not undercut the work of the minister, and they do not engage in that indoor sport known as "playing one minister off against another." They reinforce the position of the senior minister, protect him when he is vulnerable, and keep the confidences he shares.

A second common characteristic of the senior pastor's secretary is that she often is at the center of the communications network for the parish. This frequently means she can respond to many telephone inquiries without interrupting the senior minister or waiting for his return.

A third common characteristic of the top quality senior pastor's secretary is that she usually is far more than a secretary. She often holds a position that could be described as secretary/assistant to the minister/assistant program coordinator/communicator-memory bank/counselor/soother of hurt feelings/generalist.

A fourth characteristic of the best of these people is that their compensation usually includes a cash salary approximately equal to a classroom teacher's salary in the public schools, three to four weeks annual vacation, pension, health insurance occasionally, social security, sick leave, and regular applications of appreciation.

A fifth characteristic is that they often serve at the pleasure of the senior minister, not on a contract basis with the personnel committee. Their "personnel committee" (unlike other lay staff members) is the senior minister. Those who have a primary loyalty to the person *who holds the office of senior minister* often serve in the same congregation for two or three decades. Those who hold a primary loyalty to (a) the previous senior minister, (b) the congregation, (c) another minister on the staff, or (d) one or two lay leaders frequently create severe and distracting problems for a newly arrived senior minister.

Finally, several congregations of various sizes have demonstrated that one of the most effective means of guaranteeing an ineffective, unhappy, and relatively brief pastorate for a newly arrived pastor or senior minister is to provide a secretary for that pastor who (a) has been serving that congregation for decades, (b) has a primary loyalty to the congregation rather than to the person who occupies the office of pastor, (c) is a member and holds an important policy-making office and/or is married to a member who holds an important policy-making office and/or has a son or daughter who is a member and holds an important policy-making office in that congregation, or (d) retains a strong affection for the previous senior minister.

How Many Secretaries Do We Need?

One of the most frequently raised questions in very large congregations is, "How many people do we need as the support staff for the program staff?" One of the reasons that question is raised so often is that it does not have a single universal answer. There are, however, five guidelines that can be used, but it must be noted there always are exceptions to any broad guideline or generalization.

First, in general, one full-time program staff person usually requires more secretarial help than is required by three one-third time program specialists. The smaller the proportion of part-time specialists on the program staff, the larger the secretarial staff.

Second, in huge and mini-denomination churches an argument can be made on the basis of efficiency and economy for a pool of secretaries rather than assigning one secretary to each program staff member or one secretary to two program staffers. A common pattern is that a pool of three secretaries can replace four secretaries, each of whom had been assigned to provide secretarial service for one or two program staff members.

The pricetag on that option often includes (a) the program staffer must respond to telephone calls and inquiries that otherwise would be answered by that program person's secretary, (b) some program staffers begin to do their own secretarial and clerical work rather than wait for or "bother" someone in the secretarial pool, (c) questions and telephone calls that come in when the program staff person is out of the office usually must await the return of that staff member, (d) opportunities for secretaries to acquire the skills for promotion to a program position through on-the-job training are eliminated and this "satisfaction" must be replaced with some other satisfaction in the compensation package, (e) productivity often is related to loyalty and most individuals develop a greater loyalty faster to persons than to institutions, (f) the turnover rate among members of the secretarial pool usually is higher than among persons assigned as secretaries to a particular person or pair of staff members and this often has a negative impact on the institutional memory system in the church office, and (g) exclusion of the senior minister's secretary (which is almost a must) from the secretarial pool may raise intra-office interpersonal problems.

A third generalization is that if the person employed as the church business administrator carries a primary self-identification as an administrative generalist, rather than as a fiscal officer-bookkeeper, this distinction usually will require one or two additional account clerk-bookkeeper-secretarial type persons on the payroll. The self-identified fiscal officer-bookkeeper usually has a smaller staff than does the administrative generalist even when the size of the congregation and the nature of the responsibilities are the same.

A fourth generalization on support staff is that in quantitative terms the large congregation with two full-time program staff members (or the equivalent) *exclusive of music staff* usually functions best with two full-time persons carrying the clerical-secretarial-bookkeeping load. When the staff reaches seven full-time program staff positions (or the equivalent including part-time program staff) many congregations are able to function effectively with five or six full-time (or the equivalent in part-time positions) in clerical-secretarial-bookkeeping positions.

Finally, and this may be the most important of these five generalizations, the greater the emphasis by the program staff on relating to members, constituents, and prospective members on a one-to-one basis, the greater the need for more program staff members and comparatively fewer persons in secretarial positions. By contrast, the greater the emphasis by the program staff on the group life of the congregation, and especially on creating and maintaining a network of large groups, the greater the need for more support staff and fewer program staff.

For example, one congregation with a major emphasis on pastoral calling and other one-to-one relationships between staff and members has six full-time program positions (which includes four ordained ministers), two secretaries, and one bookkeeper. Another congregation of approximately the same type and size, but with a strong emphasis on small adult face-to-face groups and a moderate emphasis on large group events has five full-time program positions (which includes two ordained ministers), four secretaries, one bookkeeper, and a full-time membership secretary. The total payroll would be almost exactly the same for these two congregations, except for the fact that the second requires two more persons on the custodial staff, plus a church hostess because of the large quantity of building-centered programming.

What Other Staff Are Needed?

When the subject of staffing the large church is raised, the most difficult question to emerge usually is, "What would you recommend for a full complement of staff for a 1500-(2,000, 4,000, or 6,000) member congregation?

Two responses can be offered to such a question. The first is that it is impossible to provide a general response to that question.

The second is, "It depends."

Under this second response there are at least four major variables. The first is the gifts, talents, interests, skills, hobbies, priorities, program concerns, and style of the senior minister. The larger the congregation, the more important it is to build a staff that complements and reinforces the priorities of the senior minister. This frequently means not only a turnover of personnel during the first two or three years following the arrival of a new senior minister, it also often means several changes in job descriptions for continuing staff and major revisions of the job descriptions for persons who are being replaced.

81

Many people object to this high turnover in staff that often accompanies a change in senior ministers, but it might be more helpful to recognize that this syndrome does not represent an inherent weakness in the clergy. A more creative response is to understand it as (a) normal and predictable institutional behavior, (b) a product of the unique characteristics of the very large congregation, (c) a result of the dominance of relational values over functional concerns in staffing the large congregation, (d) an effect of the deference pyramid which causes many ministers to feel more comfortable if they have seniority over the rest of the program staff, and (e) a consequence of the new senior minister's right to build a staff team that he feels comfortable with in what to him is a new behavior setting.

A second variable in defining staff positions in the large congregation—the style of programming—was identified at the end of the previous section of this chapter. The church that places high priority on the pastoral care of members on a one-to-one basis usually will have a different mixture of staff than the congregation that places high priority on small face-to-face groups, on large group events, and on a huge variety of activities in the church building.

A third variable is the length of time the congregation has been in existence. Newer congregations usually require a smaller and less complex staff than do long established congregations. (For other related factors overlapping this third variable, see pages 59-61.)

A fourth major variable is pluralism. The more pluralistic the membership, the larger and more varied the assortment of program staff that is required. For example, the relatively homogeneous, rapidly growing, 20-year-old, 1900-member, family-centered, suburban congregation meeting in a 15-year-old building may function very comfortably with two ordained ministers, a director of Christian education, perhaps one other program specialist plus the music staff, two secretaries, and one or two custodians. By contrast, the very pluralistic, 100-year-old, 1900-member downtown church meeting in a 70-year-old building may require a staff that includes a senior pastor, an associate minister, a children's worker or a youth director, a minister of evangelism, a full-time music director, a parish visitor, a church business administrator, a director of adult ministries or a community worker, three, four, or five secretaries, a bookkeeper, and two or three custodians.

How Much Will All This Cost?

The one institutional factor that small congregations and large churches have in common is that their costs for staff are above average. It is not uncommon in small churches for the annual cost of the minister's total compensation (cash salary, pension, health insurance, utilities, housing allowance, and continuing education stipend) to average $100 to $200 per member (in terms of 1980 dollars). The lowest cost churches tend to be those averaging 150 to 180 at Sunday morning worship. In these congregations the annual cost of all staff compensation may average $60 to $120 per member or about one-half the per member cost of small congregations.

In adequately staffed large congregations averaging 300 or more at worship the total amount paid in compensation for all staff members rarely is under $100 per member and often is in the $150 to $200 per member range (in 1980 dollars). Small congregations and very large churches both spend a lot of money on staff salaries. The larger the membership, the greater the degree of pluralism, the longer the congregation has been in existence, the heavier the emphasis on program and group life, and the more widely scattered the membership, the greater the per member costs for staff salaries.

Another way of looking at this question is in terms of percentages. In the middle-sized congregation the total cost of staff compensation usually is between 25 and 45 percent of the total annual expenditure. In small churches and in very large congregations, the total cost for all staff compensation rarely is below 40 percent, often is in the 50 to 60 percent range and occasionally is in the 60 to 70 percent bracket.

These yardsticks are generalizations, and there are many exceptions. One of the major reasons for these exceptions is that the accounting systems used by many congregations and denominations make it difficult to identify staff costs. For example, in several denominations payments by churches to finance the theological education of future ministers are identified as a benevolence item rather than as a cost of staff services. By not providing for the financial support of theological seminaries, thousands of congregations in other denominations are able to minimize expenditures for staff.

A second example is that the churches using a call system of ministerial placement seldom label expenditures by the pulpit search committee or moving expenses for a new minister as a staff cost. A third example is that in many annual conferences of the United Methodist Church the costs of operating the appointment system usually are identified as "money sent away," rather than as staff costs. In addition, in many conferences large United Methodist congregations are expected to pay (a) part of the current costs for pensions of ministers now retired, (b) the pension costs for their own staff, and (c) part of the pension costs for pastors serving smaller congregations. This makes it difficult to calculate the full amount of current staff costs.

An even more complex, and far more important subject in staffing the large church is the development of the appropriate model of staff relationships, and that deserves a separate chapter.

CHAPTER THREE
Models of Staff Relationships

"I've had five associates in the nine years I've been at Grace Church and only two of them really earned what we paid them," observed the fifty-seven-year-old senior minister of that 725-member congregation, as he chatted with several other pastors late one evening. These busy pastors had gathered for a three-day workshop planned for the senior ministers of large congregations. After the evening session had ended, seven of them had adjourned to a lounge to relax in comfortable chairs, renew acquaintances, meet new friends, partake of refreshments, share experiences, swap lies, and exchange old war stories. "The unfortunate part is that neither one of the two good ones stayed more than two years," he continued. "We always go to the seminary for our associates, and these two both wanted the experience of working in a big church before going out on their own. A third, who was slightly above average, stayed nearly three years, but I was willing to see him go when he announced he was leaving."

"Our staff is one big happy family," boasted the senior minister of the 1900-member Trinity Church. "There are seven of us—me, two associates, the DCE, a minister of music, the business manager, and my administrative assistant. We meet for two or three hours every Tuesday afternoon, and we have two overnight staff retreats every year. I hear other pastors complaining about staff problems, but we don't have any of that at Trinity. Each one of our staff members truly loves every other person on the staff, and we really take care of one another. Sometimes interpersonal concerns take up most of a staff meeting and we don't get much business taken care of, but it's worth the hour or two it takes every week in order to have a staff that works together as a team."

"According to what I heard even before I got there, the church I'm serving had never been able to develop a unified and cohesive staff," observed the senior minister of Redeemer Church, "but we have one now. There are four of us on the program staff, and we meet for two hours as a staff twice a week. Some of the leaders think we spend too much time in staff meetings, but we believe we need it. Redeemer has had a reputation for years of being a parish that is hard on staff, and some of the members do give us a rough time, but we hang together. One reason we meet twice a week is that together we are a support group for ourselves. When I first came, five years ago, I was told that I would be doing well if I lasted three years. I think that prediction might have been fulfilled if I hadn't been able to build a strong, supportive staff."

"I've always believed in delegating both responsibility and authority," declared the pastor from Bethel Church and the senior member of the group. "I now have a staff of five and everyone is both able and willing to accept responsibility and to follow through. We meet for an hour to an hour and a half once a week to check signals, clear the calendar, coordinate program, and keep one another informed. Sometimes two or three days will pass and I won't even see a couple of the other staff members. I carry my share of the load and they carry theirs."

"We have staff meetings at all hours of the day and night," offered the only woman in the group, with a smile, "in bed, during meals, in the car, while we're cleaning house as well as in the office." As she spoke, she reached over and took the hand of her husband who was sitting next to her. "Jack and I are the copastors at Wood Memorial Church. Except for a part-time seminary student who is our youth director and a part-time choir director-organist, we're the whole program staff. It sometimes seems that we spend a lot more time in staff meetings than we spend in family meetings."

"When I came to my present situation the congregation had set it up as a copastorate and it's working out real well," bragged the 48-year-old pastor from First Church. "Four years before my predecessor resigned, they had called as their new associate a bright young man fresh out of seminary. He's a great preacher, considerably better than my predecessor was, a good teacher, and has a wonderful personality. The congregation didn't want to lose him, so he served as the interim minister during the vacancy period. After negotiations with two other candidates fell through, they revised the job descriptions and abolished the positions of senior pastor and associate minister. They replaced them with two positions each called copastor and promoted the young associate to one of these and called me to the other. I've been there almost a year now, and it's working beautifully. We split everything right down the middle. I preach twenty-six Sundays a year and he preaches twenty-six."

"Who preaches on Easter and Christmas Sundays?" inquired one of the other ministers.

"I do," replied the copastor. "The pulpit nominating committee insisted that I have first choice of the Sundays that I preach since I am older. I agreed since I can't imagine what I would do if I weren't in the pulpit on Palm Sunday and Easter."

"Oh, you also preach on Palm Sunday," commented another member of the group. "How do your salaries compare?"

"Naturally I receive a higher salary," came the reply. "After all, I'm older, I have more experience, two of our children are in high school and one is in college and it simply costs us more to live. But that doesn't make any difference in our relationship. We still see ourselves as equal partners."

"One of my associates is eleven years older than I am and has a dozen years more experience in the parish ministry than I have," commented the senior minister at Redeemer Church, "but my cash salary is approximately $7,000 more than his. I have a hunch that if your members pay you considerably more than they pay your younger colleague, most of them believe you are really the senior minister in that arrangement."

These comments illustrate two very important aspects of staff relationships. The first is that senior ministers usually place the quality of staff relationships much higher on the list than do the other members of the same staff. In general, senior ministers are less dissatisfied with the quality of staff relationships than are the other ministers on the staff so they tend to project a comparatively favorable image of the quality of staff relationships.[1] This may be one reason why senior pastors tend to be less interested than associate ministers in a discussion of the various models of staff relationships.

The second point illustrated by this conversation is the subject of this chapter. There are a variety of models of staff relationships and the choice of model influences performance, tenure, and roles as well as interpersonal and professional relationships.

Every model is based on a conceptual framework of the place of paid professional staff persons in the parish and of their relationships with the laity. Frequently this conceptual framework or perspective has never been articulated, even though it is a product of value systems and has a tremendous impact on the model chosen.

Which Perspective?

There are at least three perspectives that can be used in looking at the multiple staff of a congregation. One that is almost completely foreign to the conceptual framework or experiences of most large Christian churches on this continent can be found in some congregations that trace their heritage back to the Anabaptist movement that surfaced in Europe during the first part of the sixteenth century. One of the denominations that has emerged from this Anabaptist tradition is the General Conference Mennonite Church, with nearly 400 congregations in the United States and Canada. Several General Conference congregations, as well as a number of churches affiliated with the (Old) Mennonite Church, illustrate this first perspective. Several Mennonite congregations developed a multiple-staff model that included bishops and two, three, or more ordained ministers. All members of this multiple staff were members of the congregation and served without financial compensation. During the last few decades many of these congregations have changed to a staff consisting of (a) one ordained minister, who serves on a full-time basis and is adequately compensated for these services and (b) one or more ordained members of the congregation who serve on a part-time basis as part of the ministerial team but without financial compensation.

This approach to a multiple staff or team ministry merits attention here because it illustrates the concept of the ministry of the laity. It also is an approach that has avoided some of the effects of professionalism that characterize the multiple staff arrangements in many large Protestant churches. However, it has provoked a few disagreements over authority and role.

A second perspective can be traced back to Cyprian, Bishop of Carthage in the third century, who brought a lawyer's perspective to theology and church administration. Cyprian insisted that the clergy be set apart from the laity, not only by ordination, but also by office, place in the institutional hierarchy, and vestments. This sharp separation of the professionals from the laity is the basic approach used for developing models for multiple staffs in most large Christian churches, both Protestant and Catholic, on this continent today.[2]

A third perspective is articulated by Robert C. Worley who has described a three-stage evolution.[3] Worley suggests that for centuries Western society has operated on a hierarchical pyramid derived from feudalism which called for a passive role for the followers. Feudalism is dead, and today's voluntary associations are filled with active people who will not support the old feudal pyramid. Worley contends that the social structure for ministry has moved from (a) one that called for a highly individualistic role for the pastor, who would lead a collection of passive individuals, to (b) an emphasis on the role of the pastor as an enabler of the group life of the parish, to (c) one that calls for the pastor to help the members build a sense of community and to help them see themselves as a called out community, rather than a collection of individuals or a coalition of groups. This third stage provides a radically different social structure for a multiple staff than is found in either the individualistic emphasis or the coalition of groups concept.

These three perspectives constitute a useful background for looking at a variety of operational models. One reason why it is important to have a conceptual framework for looking at models of multiple staff relationships is that it is far easier to build an effective model if every participant shares the same frame of reference. Many staff conflicts over models can be traced to differences in perspective.

A second reason for reflecting on perspective is change. Too often efforts to develop a new model for staff relationships fail because the proposed change is from one model that is compatible with one perspective and the new model proposed is compatible with a different conceptual framework or perspective. Unless a change is made in the conceptual framework, it will be very difficult to replace the old model with a new model. Frequently major changes are required in the entire organizational context including the denominational system of ministerial placement, the structure of congregational self-government, the operational theological assumptions of everyone involved, and the various traditions of staff roles in that congregation. One example of the compatibility problem is when a congregation, following the perspective defined by Cyprian and his successors, seeks to develop a leadership model that emphasizes the equal participation of both lay volunteers and paid professional staff members. That model is reasonably consistent with the Anabaptist tradition found in many Mennonite congregations today, but it is incompatible with the monarchial hierarchy that dominates the traditions of most North American Protestant and Catholic denominations. Another example is the concept of the copastorate, which is compatible with the perspective set forth by Robert C. Worley, but incompatible with the traditional hierarchy that is part of the tradition of most large Christian churches.

A third, and perhaps the most important reason for looking at these differences in perspective is the matter of evaluation. What is the best approach for a church to follow in building an organizational structure for staff relationships? There is no specific and universal response to such a question. The "right" answer is that the model should reflect and be consistent with the values and goals of the participants. Those seeking a distinctively "Christian" model can develop an impressive historical case for arguing that the monarchial hierarchy pioneered by Cyprian is *the* Christian perspective. Opponents of that position, however, can develop a very impressive biblical and theological rationale for either of the other two perspectives. Or to shift to a denominational example, Methodists can, by a selective reading of their unique history, develop an impressive case that any one of the three perspectives is the distinctly Methodist position, although most of the practices follow the Cyprian approach.

With the context of these three perspectives the discussion now can turn to operational models of multiple staff relationships, most of which are consistent with the monarchial hierarchy endorsed by Cyprian.

What Are Models?

The comments quoted at the beginning of this chapter can be used to introduce a discussion of models since each senior pastor reflected a different model of staff relationships.

The pastor from Grace Church, who had worked with five associates in nine years, described one of the more widely used models. Various surveys suggest that between one-fourth and one-third of all associate ministers are (1) in their first full-time pastoral position or (2) in an intern year between the second and third year of their seminary training and (3) under thirty-two years of age.

The usual model of this arrangement parallels that of the master craftsman-apprentice relationships that have been used for centuries to train carpenters, masons, physicians, lawyers, police officers, pastors, mechanics, plumbers, and other artisans. The persistence of this instructional model over hundreds of years suggests that it must have relevance or it would not have survived. Today it is much more widely used in the training of Roman Catholic priests than with Protestant ministers.

The usual format is for the older, experienced, and skilled practitioner to teach the younger apprentice the knowledge and skills necessary for that vocation. The apprentice begins with very limited responsibilities and serves more as a "flunky," helper, or observer at first. Gradually the responsibilities of the apprentice are increased until he or she is ready for certification as a journeyman. The usual custom in Protestant churches is to use this model to convey to the young seminary graduate the skills, insights, and wisdom necessary to function effectively as a junior member of the program staff in a large and complex congregation with tremendous resources, and, after two or three years, for that young minister to move on to become the pastor of a much smaller and radically different type of congregation.

The senior minister at Trinity Church described that staff as "one big happy family" and went on to describe what might be defined as a relational model. While most of the staff members carry functional titles, the emphasis appears to be on relationships rather than on functions or performance.

Or, it could be that the model used at Trinity Church resembles most closely a third approach to multiple staff relationships. This widely used model can be identified simply as "the one big family." The senior minister, who typically is in the 35 to 55 age bracket and substantially younger than his predecessor, acts as the father figure. The older associate minister, who is approaching final retirement, is the grandfather in this model. He is proud and very protective of his "son" the senior minister, but occasionally he privately voices disagreement with the senior minister's program priorities, theological stance, leadership style, allocation of time, choice of lay leadership, or selection of other staff members. Despite these modest private disagreements, however, this older associate minister is always publicly supportive of the senior minister both in public statements and in his actions.

The mother role in this model usually is filled by the secretary to the senior minister or by the woman who serves as the administrative assistant to the senior pastor, if she is older than the senior minister or if she has had longer tenure. She attends staff meetings and has seniority over most of the other staff members. In other situations this role may be filled by the veteran parish worker, the longtime choir director, the organist, the financial secretary, the director of Christian education, or the part-time female staff member who edits the church newsletter and oversees the internal communication system of the parish.

The "children" in this model usually are drawn from the younger members of the program staff who have been serving that congregation for only a year or two or three. They may include the young associate minister who graduated from seminary a year or two ago and is in her first full-time position, the male associate in his late 20s, the young director of Christian education, the youth director, or the new young minister of music.

One of the parallels with the biological family is that the parents and grandparents usually take a more favorable perspective on the quality of the interpersonal relationships than is taken by the younger members of the family, some of whom are ready to leave "home" at the first favorable opportunity in the hope of finding a less paternalistic environment.

A fourth model is reflected in the comments of the senior minister from Redeemer Church. He noted that Redeemer had a reputation for being "hard on staff." This is not a rare comment, and a common response is to use an ancient organizing principle to turn a loose collection of individuals into a closely knit, cohesive, and unified group. The staff finds a sense of unity by organizing against the enemy, and the enemy is the congregation. When this happens, the conversation at staff meetings often includes numerous third person pronouns, and the "theys," "thems," and "theirs" refer to the congregation.

A fifth and very widely used model can be identified in the remarks of the senior minister from Bethel Church who declared that he likes to delegate responsibility and authority. This is primarily a functional model, in contrast to the relational emphasis at Trinity Church. The functional model usually is characterized by (a) a strong, directive, and hard-working senior minister who thinks in functional and professional terms, (b) a heavy emphasis on job descriptions, (c) an organizational structure for the congregation that places the basic responsibility for program development and the implementation of policy decisions on functional committees such as education, finance, trustees, worship, evangelism, social action, *et al.* (in contrast to a structure that is organized around events and activities or one that is based on people and their distinctive needs), (d) staff members are assigned to the various functional committees and therefore naturally develop a strong identification with and loyalty to their task and committee, and (e) the assumption that each staff member has the basic staff responsibility for that committee. The staff comes together for meetings, less as a central staff, but more as a meeting of staff representatives from the several organizational substructures of the congregation. Each staff member is expected to represent, and if necessary, to defend his or her "turf" and the interests of that constituency. The basic purposes of the staff meeting are communication, coordination, updating the calendar, and other functional concerns.

This is a relatively impersonal model. When one staff member leaves, a committee hires someone to fill the vacant position and to assume its responsibilities rather than seeking a replacement and then reassigning responsibilities according to the gifts and talents of what has become a new team.

This model has much to commend it in terms of productivity, the endorsement of many older business-oriented lay persons, and the clarity of responsibilities. The price tag on these advantages is that it definitely is in the Cyprian tradition with the senior minister in the role of "bishop." This model rarely produces long tenure among staff members born since 1940 who are more relationally oriented. Each staff member usually has to build his or her own support group. The pastoral relations committee may act as the support group for the senior minister, but rarely is it able to serve as an effective support group for the other staff members. (Renaming it, as many United Methodist congregations have done, as "The Staff-Parish Relations

Committee," rarely solves that problem and usually only creates the illusion that no problem exists). Each staff member has to build his or her own support group or go without. In this model the staff meetings are largely concerned with "business," not personal concerns.

While many senior ministers born before 1935 find this to be a very comfortable and productive model after they have developed it, many newly arrived senior ministers, regardless of age, find themselves frustrated by it. One reason is that the ministerial selection process usually promised the candidate complete freedom in building a new staff, but after arrival, the new senior minister finds each program staff member represents a constituency with (a) considerable clout and (b) a conviction that if "our" staff person is demoted or dismissed or reassigned that symbolizes a loss of prestige for "our" committee or program. Like other bishops have learned over the centuries, the newly arrived senior minister in this model may soon discover that he has tremendous power, as long as he does not attempt to exercise it.

While it is still relatively rare, a sixth model may represent a substantial part of tomorrow's scene. Today there are scores of husband-wife teams, both of whom are physicians or lawyers or accountants, who have set themselves up in private practice as a partnership. The number of these professional partnerships is increasing. A parallel, which is just beginning to appear on the scene, is the husband-wife team who share pastoral responsibilities in a large congregation. (There are several dozen of these "clergy couples" sharing the pastoral work in small or middle-sized churches or in two or three church parishes, but the seniority and experience "rules" have thus far kept to a small number the husband-wife teams in large congregations.) One of the most frequently-heard comments from ministers in this model is the difficulty of isolating professional and church concerns to leave time for personal and family time.

One of the most widely promoted and discussed models is the copastorate. This was described by the recently arrived copastor at First Church in the opening section of this chapter. The questions raised by his colleagues on salary and preaching schedule underscore two of the many reasons why this model is widely discussed but rarely encountered. The basic reason for its comparative scarcity is that it usually is incompatible with the Cyprian perspective and few churches have turned Worley's perspective into an operational pattern. The copastorate is compatible with Worley's conceptual framework, but it cannot be imposed on the Cyprian model which allows for only one "bishop" per congregation. A set of secondary reasons for its scarcity can be found in the last chapter of this volume.

The copastor model tends to be more likely to succeed in those large congregations that (a) are severely understaffed, (b) are organized on a functional, rather than on a relational basis, (c) are highly liturgical with a great emphasis on the Eucharist, (d) employ two ministers of approximately the same age and who represent the same value system, (e) provide equal compensation for the two ministers, (f) place a high value on the office of pastor, rather than on who holds that office and (g) do not have a history of one domineering senior minister.

Another model, although it is relatively rare, deserves attention because it illustrates one approach to staff relationships.

At St. Matthew's Church the hard-working, task-oriented, serious, and ambitious senior minister spends the equivalent of eight to ten weeks every year with denominational boards and committees. The 39-year-old associate minister is enrolled, on a part-time basis, in graduate school in a program which will lead to the Ph. D. degree in another four or five years. The director of Christian education is serving the second year of a very satisfying two-year term as president of the national fellowship of Christian educators in that denomination. The 26-year-old associate minister is heavily involved in community ministries to residents of the neighborhood, hardly any of whom are members of St. Matthew's, and in ecumenical committees and programs.

When interviewed, each of the four insists the relationships among them are excellent and that there are no staff tensions or jealousies or frictions. Why does this model produce such a utopian response? All staff members have a major "outside" interest that consumes large quantities of time, energy, and creativity and their "part-time" employment at St. Matthew's does not allow for staff conflicts. No one has a parish turf to protect.

Other models include (a) the "fellow ranchers" in which one minister works one end of the ranch, the second works the other end, so they have no basis for conflict, although the middle part of the ranch may be neglected, (b) the staff in which two or three or four of the members are competitors and antagonists, rather than partners, and at staff meetings the rest of the staff quietly and passively watch the competition for place and prestige, (c) the "carbon copy" in which the senior minister has chosen program staff members who are notable for their close resemblance to the senior minister's skills, gifts, talents, values, and priorities (and sometimes even physical appearance), (d) the complementary staff in which each one of the individual staff members has a distinctive set of gifts and talents that complement, rather than duplicate, the gifts and talents of the other members of the staff and everyone, staff and members alike, know by these gifts and talents who is the logical staff member to turn to for a specific concern or need, (e) the "fun" model in which each person on the staff greatly enjoys his or her own responsibilities *and* enjoys being with the other members of the staff *and* enjoys being on the staff of that particular called-out community of Christians, and (f) the four ordained-minister staff, consisting of a senior minister and one associate who are very close both personally and professionally, a second associate minister who is professionally very competent, but tends to remain somewhat aloof in interpersonal relationships with the rest of the staff, and the third associate minister who either is looking for a clearer role on that staff but has not yet found it or is in a "rest and rehabilitation" stage between the last church and the next one.

Which model, or combination of models, comes closest to describing the staff relationships in your congregation? What are the advantages of that model? What are the disadvantages? How could it be improved? Most important of all, do all of the staff members agree on which model is being followed?

Contract or Covenant?

Another approach to looking at staff relationships is in the distinction between a contract and a covenant. Many large congregations prepare a job description, seek someone to fill that position, and "contract" with one candidate to fill that position and carry out those responsibilities. Frequently the contract has an "escape clause" which provides the method by which either party may terminate the contract unilaterally. Sometimes a personnel committee is the group representing the congregation with authority to negotiate changes in the contract with each staff member.

By contrast, a covenant creates a community of interest with a much greater emphasis on personal relationships and caring for one another. In his writings Paul identified a violation of the covenant as an offense against the Lord (I Cor. 11:27-32) which is far different from breaking a civil contract. The Old Testament is filled with an array of laws and contracts. The New Testament is the story of a new covenant.

When a church employs someone to repair the sidewalk, that is a contract. When that same congregation employs an associate minister or a director of Christian education, is that a contract or a covenant?

It is crucial that all persons on the payroll of the large congregation understand whether they are in a contract or covenant relationship with the church. The name we use influences the expectations of all parties to the arrangement. It also determines whether the contract can be terminated by the unilateral action of one party or whether termination must be a bilateral decision. In recent years in American society there has been a gradual shift in the direction of identifying marriage as a contract rather than a covenant.

Many congregations symbolize this distinction through an installation service for those persons on the staff who have a covenant relationship with that called-out community. Others symbolize it by providing, formally or informally, a support group for staff members in a covenant relationship, but not for those in a contractual relationship.

What is the relationship between each staff person and the congregation in your parish? A covenant or a contract? Does everyone involved agree on the name and on the implications of that choice of name? Clarifying this distinction is important to an understanding of role.

What Is My Role?

The more clearly defined the role of a staff member, the more likely that person will enjoy meaningful satisfactions from filling that role and the less likely that person will encounter frustrations because of confusion over role.

The difficulty with that simple generalization is that in most large congregations only a few members of the staff have reasonably clearly defined roles. These may include the senior minister (unless the senior minister is one of the newest members of the staff), the female director of Christian education, the semi-retired minister of visitation, the youth director (occasionally), the choir director, the organist, and the bookkeeper. These are the staff roles that most often have been institutionalized. When a new person joins the staff and moves into one of these roles, it is reasonable to expect (a) the new staff member will have a clear understanding of his or her role, (b) the rest of the staff will have a clear understanding of the new person's role, and (c) the members of the congregation will have a reasonably clear understanding of the new employee's role and of what to expect of that new staff member.

The most notable omission from this list is the associate minister, and that is one reason why a chapter of this book is reserved for that position.

In broad general terms, the basic implication of this issue is that the quality of staff relationships will depend to a substantial degree on the active cooperation of those staff members who have a clearly defined role in understanding the institutional pressures on the fellow staff member who does not have a clearly defined role and in helping to clarify the role of that colleague. The next chapter includes an explanation of why the senior minister is at the top of the list of those responsible for helping this to happen and a suggestion on how to do it.

What Are the Expectations?

Overlapping this question on role is the issue of the expectations the congregation places on the staff and the expectation the senior minister has of the other members of the program staff. Is it expected that the employed staff will "do" the work? Or is it expected that the staff will cause things to happen? Traditionally the common expectation has been that the staff will "take charge" and do everything. This is still a widespread assumption on the part of both lay leaders and employed staff in many congregations. Perhaps the most common example is to employ a director of Christian education who becomes the paid Sunday school superintendent. Frequently an ordained minister is called to do parish visitation. Or a staff person is employed to do youth ministries.

A growing pattern, however, is to seek staff members who are responsible for causing things to happen, rather than doing everything. Four examples will illustrate this concept. In one congregation it was decided that a high priority would be to give the high school youth a chance to be with a variety of models of adult Christians. The assignment for the part-time youth director was to recruit and train a dozen adults to serve as a team of counselors for the youth program. In another church, which felt it was very short of lay volunteers, a lay woman was employed on a part-time basis to identify, recruit, train, help place, and provide the personal support for potential workers and leaders. In a third parish a lay woman was secured on a one-third time basis to organize lay visitation teams and to recruit and train individuals who would help new adult members "find a home" in one of the groups, circles, classes, committees, organizations, and boards in that parish. In a rapidly growing congregation a lay person was employed on a three-quarter time basis to see that group life expanded as the membership increased. Each of these four staff members was employed with precise and clearly defined responsibilities to expand the program and to involve lay volunteers in that effort. Each was a specialist rather than a generalist.

There is some reason to believe that when a congregation adds another ordained minister to the staff, the members expect that person to do the work, but are willing to accept a lay staff person as a "partner" or "enabler" who has the responsibility to see that the job gets done, rather than the staff person doing everything by herself or himself.

In general, the clearer the expectations on this distinction between "doing it" and "causing it to happen," the better the quality of staff morale and relationships.

What Is the Influence of Birth Order?

While it is only a minor consideration in the total context of staff relationships, the most widely neglected factor in building a model of staff relationships is birth order. During the past dozen years a huge amount of research has been completed that suggests a person's place in the family constellation is an influential factor in the personal characteristics of 70–80 percent of the adult population.[4]

First-born children, for example, tend to be conscientious, task-oriented, persistent, serious, high-achievers, holders of high expectations of others, in occupations and professions that provide a surrogate parent role, comfortable giving orders to others, and inclined to develop hierarchically-oriented schemas for ordering reality.

Middle-born children tend to be more person-centered, relaxed, diplomatic, friendly, skilled in getting along with other people, and likely to smile very easily.

Last borns tend to be relaxed, very casual in dress and appearance, playful, lighthearted, able to ignore that which does not interest them and to concentrate on those tasks and concerns that do interest them, and willing to accept a subordinate position, and they often express a great interest in change.[5]

Interviews by this writer with members of the multiple staffs in 296 large congregations suggest that research on birth order has something to say to staff relationships. Six observations can be offered here to support that suggestion. First, like other ruling elders such as kings, presidents, and physicians, senior ministers are drawn in statistically disproportionately large numbers from among first-borns.

A second pattern that emerged from this survey is that a disproportionately large number of multiple staffs composed of two or more ordained ministers include two or more first-born ministers. Third, the least happy arrangements tend to be those that include two or more first-born staff members or an only-born senior minister and an only-born associate. (This second combination turned out to be so rare as to be statistically insignificant.) Fourth, the happiest staff combinations tend to be those that include a middle-born senior minister and a middle-born associate minister. Fifth, while comparatively rare, the most relaxed and the least competitive staff teams include a last-born senior pastor and a last-born associate minister. Finally, the most effective ministerial teams tend to be composed of a middle-born senior minister and a first-born associate.

If all the factors used in selecting a candidate for a position on a multiple staff have a combined value of one hundred points, in perhaps three cases out of four the birth-order factor should be given a weight of ten to twenty points. With the other one-fourth of the candidates birth order probably deserves a weight of zero to five points in selecting members of a multiple staff team.

Who Does the Getting Along?

In the happiest two-pastor multiple staff teams the senior pastor does perhaps 80 percent of the "getting along" with the associate and the associate minister does about 80 percent of the "getting along" with the senior pastor. The result is a surplus of getting along. In the unhappy arrangements each contributes 10–20 percent to that process and the resulting deficit produces unhappiness.[6]

This raises the question of who has the responsibility to provide a disproportionately large amount of the "getting along with the other" ingredient in multiple staff arrangements. In general, while they may be unfair, seven patterns have emerged in our culture that bear on this issue. Younger persons are expected to get along with older persons. The newest member of a group is expected to get along and to make the necessary adjustments to fit into the ongoing set of interpersonal relationships that have developed among the other members of that group. Lay people are expected to get along with clergy. Women generally have more experience in getting along with men than men have in getting along with men. Middle-borns have more experience in getting along with other persons than do first-borns. First-borns tend to expect other people to get along with them. Associate ministers are expected to get along with senior pastors.

One translation of the birth-order factor is that if the newest member of a staff is a young, middle-born lay woman she will be expected to get along with the other members of the group—and she will feel very comfortable doing that. A second translation is that if the new associate minister is an older first-born ordained male, he may not understand that the basic responsibility for getting along with the other members of the staff in general, and with the senior minister in particular, rests on him—and he also may regard this as an unfair assumption. (This is one of the reasons why associate ministers usually express a lower level of satisfaction with the quality of staff relationships than do senior pastors.)

In other words, it helps to know what the rules are, and it is essential for anyone seeking to change them to know the rules.

What Are the Seven C's?

In building a model of staff relationships or in evaluating an existing model, it may be useful to look at seven criteria. These seven criteria are compatibility, continuity, competence, confidence, coherence, complementarity, and the conceptualization of the role and purpose of that particular congregation. The first represents the need for both personal *and* professional compatibility among the members of the staff team. The second emphasizes the importance of long term relationships and long pastorates. While there is no evidence that long pastorates produce church growth, nearly all of today's rapidly growing congregations, *which sustain that growth,* have long pastorates. The third criterion represents the obvious need for competence in the professional leadership of the large congregation.

The fourth reflects the confidence the members of the congregation have in the paid staff. The fifth word, coherence, reflects a programmatic consistency among the staff members as they display a logically connected set of professional relationships. One evidence of this is when each program or ministry reinforces agreed-upon priorities in fulfilling the role God has called that congregation to accept. The sixth word, complementary, describes how the staff members complement one another and thus make a fully rounded team covering a wide variety of perspectives and needs. This is in contrast to a more common pattern of picking an associate minister who is a younger carbon copy of the senior pastor. The final term refers to the way in which the staff members conceptualize the purpose, nature, and role of that congregation. Is there a high degree of agreement on that definition? Do the various concepts of purpose and role complement or compete with one another?

These are seven yardsticks for a collective evaluation of a staff team. When a staff team scores high on six or seven of the seven, it is unlikely that changes in personnel will improve the score!

CHAPTER FOUR
The Senior Minister

"How do you fellows manage your time?" inquired Howard Jones of two other ministers, as the three were traveling together in Howard's automobile to a denominational meeting. "This is my first experience as the senior pastor in a large congregation with a professional staff, and it seems that from the first day I arrived at First Church I have found myself short of time. There simply aren't enough hours in a day to do everything I have to do. You both have had years of experience as senior ministers, how do you handle these pressures on your time?"

"That's a fair question, Howard, but it shouldn't be your number one concern," replied Burt Hanson who was in the seventh year of his second experience as the senior minister of a large parish. "After about five years of never having enough hours in the day in my first hitch as a senior pastor, I finally woke up one day and decided that I was fighting the wrong battle. For five years I had been trying to choose between what I did and what I delegated to others. I always picked too much to do myself, and the result was I was always short of time. One day I decided that if I could define my role more clearly other things would fall into place. I suggest you forget about the time pressures and begin to think about defining your role as the senior minister at First Church. After you have done that, you can set the priorities that will enable you to manage your time. Until you define your role, you can't set priorities, and you can't manage your time effectively unless you have a feel for your priorities."

"I would agree with Burt, I believe," added Jim Turner, the third member of the group. "But there is another issue you have to think about and that is style. We're all different, and there is no one leadership style that fits all pastors, but after you have decided on the leadership style you are comfortable with, it will be easier to respond to the pressures of the clock and the calendar and to set your priorities."

This conversation illustrates three different facets of the discussion about the senior minister in the large church. Such a discussion could begin with what a senior minister does and does not do or with an analysis of the unique role of the senior minister in a large parish or with an evaluation of alternative leadership styles.

If one accepts two of the basic assumptions on which this book is based, however, there is only one logical beginning point for looking at the office of senior minister. The first assumption, which constitutes the theme of the first chapter, is that the larger congregation is a unique religious organization and is not simply an overgrown version of the typical church. The second basic assumption is that the larger church provides a distinctive behavior setting that has a tremendous influence on the role, leadership style, duties, and allocation of time by the senior minister. Therefore, the logical beginning point is to look first at the role of the senior pastor in the larger church. Perhaps the best way of doing this is to return to the anthropological analogy of the tribe that was introduced near the middle of the first chapter and to elaborate on that analogy. For purposes of analysis and discussion, it may help to divide the position of senior minister into three roles— the number one medicine man, the tribal chief, and the chief administrative officer of the congregation.

Who Is the Tribal Chief?

In most larger congregations the senior minister is, and should be, the tribal chief, the number one medicine man, and the chief administrative officer. This often is more difficult than it first appears.

One reason it is difficult is that many newly arrived ministers come from one or more pastorates in which the ordained minister was the medicine man for the smaller family, clan, or tribe, but the office of tribal chief always was filled by a layperson. In the majority of all Protestant congregations on this continent the combination of denominational polity and local customs, such as a tradition of short pastorates, have reserved the role of tribal chief for a layperson. Thus after five, ten, or twenty years experience specializing as a medicine man, the pastor, with considerable experience as a medicine man and no experience as a tribal chief, moves on to become the senior pastor of a large church. The members of the large congregation know the new senior minister should fill the role of tribal chief that was left vacant when the previous senior pastor departed. The newly arrived senior minister knows, on the basis of years of pastoral experience in smaller congregations, plus perhaps what had been taught in seminary, that a layperson always acts as the chief of the tribe. The usual result is considerable frustration on the part of everyone involved in leadership.

A second, but less common reason can be found in some large congregations using the call system of ministerial placement (that category includes dozens of United Methodist congregations) in which there has been a long vacancy period since the departure of the last senior pastor/chief medicine man/tribal chief. The position of senior minister is still vacant, but an associate minister, who has been on the staff for several years, has gradually moved into the position of the chief medicine man and a longtime lay member has begun to exercise the prerogatives of tribal chief. The new senior minister comes on the scene after the long vacancy period to find only the least influential of the three offices to be vacant.

A third reason why it may be difficult for some senior ministers to fill all three offices is that many ordained ministers are convinced by both their call to preach the gospel and their training that their role is to be preacher, not a medicine man or a tribal chief. Those who have a genuine and sincere conviction that this is their call probably should concentrate on serving family and clan-type churches and avoid becoming the pastor of a tribe or nation.

Finally, there are four other large church patterns which, while relatively uncommon, do not offer a vacant office of tribal chief to be filled by the newly arrived senior minister. The first pattern is that in a few large congregations, usually those with a strong sense of congregational autonomy, the custom for years has been for a layperson to fill the role of tribal chief. The second is the congregation that for many years has endured what the members perceive to be the tyranny of a very autocratic senior minister, and these members have decided that never again will they entrust the office of tribal chief to the person who holds the office of senior minister. The third exception is the large church in which the office of tribal chief was taken over some years ago by the minister of music, the career associate minister, the church business administrator, or the director of Christian education. The fourth is when the former pastor, who occupied the offices of senior minister, chief medicine man, and tribal chief for two or three decades, retires, resigns the office of senior minister, and perhaps surrenders most of the prerogatives that go with being chief medicine man, but continues to live in the community, function as a member of that congregation, and hang on to the position of tribal chief.

In summary, one of the first questions a senior minister must ask about his role is, "Do I want to be the tribal chief here?" The vast majority of members of large, huge, and minidenomination-sized churches are convinced that the only acceptable answer to that question is yes! Even in most of the circumstances mentioned above where no vacancy exists, many, and usually most, lay leaders expect the newly arrived senior minister to take the initiative in creating a vacancy and filling it.

It must be recognized, however, that in some situations the senior minister cannot have zero interest in serving in that role. Therefore, in reviewing the role of the senior minister in the large church, it becomes necessary to ask four additional questions.

What Does the Tribal Chief Do?

Regardless of who holds the office of tribal chief, there are certain powers and obligations that go with that office. It may help to sharpen the definition of the role of the senior minister to look at a dozen of these responsibilities of the tribal chief.

1. The tribal chief speaks first when meeting other members of the tribe. Extroverted, outgoing, and gregarious members rarely notice this, and some do not even give the chief the opportunity to speak first, but the shy, bashful, introverted, and timid members are deeply appreciative of this leadership characteristic of the tribal chief.

2. The tribal chief calls the members by name when meeting them. For the tribal chief to remember the name of every member of that huge tribe impresses the members. Most of them are flattered and all are grateful that the chief knows them by name.

3. The tribal chief remembers and inquires about the health or the progress or the whereabouts of children, spouses, and parents whenever meeting members of the tribe.

4. The tribal chief knows and understands the special burdens being carried by some especially troubled members of the tribe *and does not conceal the fact that the chief knows and cares.*

5. The tribal chief sees the climate of optimism or pessimism that will influence the decision-making processes of the tribe.

6. The tribal chief projects a vision of what the tribe could become in the days and years ahead. This may be either a positive or a negative vision.

7. The tribal chief frames the questions or sets the agenda, states the diagnosis or defines the problem that will influence the direction the tribe will take as it looks into the future.

The definition of the problem or the content of the diagnostic statement has a tremendous influence on the resulting prescription for action. (John Kenneth Galbraith goes a step farther and contends that the remedy prescribes the diagnosis.[1]) The tribal chief recognizes that there are no neutral definitions of the problem, or diagnosis, and is willing to accept the responsibility for taking the initiative in defining the issues facing the tribe.

8. The tribal chief does not hesitate to express his or her own values and goals and seeks to have these adopted as tribal values and goals.

9. The tribal chief defines the rules of the planning and decision-making games that will be played in the tribe.

10. The tribal chief, partly because of the authority of the office, partly as a result of hard work, and partly because of a willingness to accept the role, gives or withholds permission on proposed changes in tribal customs, schedules, priorities, celebrations, and allocation of scarce resources. (A simple translation is that the tribal chief is a political power.)

11. The tribal chief makes sure that sacred tribal customs are honored and that tribal holidays are celebrated.

12. The tribal chief is concerned about reinforcing the loyalty of the members to the tribe with special emphasis on the younger members of the tribe and new members.

These are among the more common responsibilities of the tribal chief in large churches. Some readers may be diverted from the issue by their value judgments about some of the items on this list. Some senior ministers may be diverted and respond negatively to some items with "I don't want to do that!" Those are diversionary responses! The critical issue is not the content of this list. The actual issue consists of two questions. First, if the senior minister does not accept the responsibilities for these and other duties of the tribal chief, who will? Second, if these duties are not discharged, what will happen to the tribe?

This may create a dilemma for the senior minister who asks, "If I don't want to be tribal chief, and if no one else accepts the responsibility for these duties, what should I do?" The best response is, either accept the role of tribal chief or make sure the duties are carried out by someone else. The remaining alternative is the deterioration of the tribe as a religious organization if the obligations and responsibilities of the office of tribal chief are left unfulfilled.

What Does the Number One Medicine Man Do?

If a distinction is made between the office of chief medicine man and tribal chief in the large church, and if the senior minister is willing and able to accept the first role but is unwilling or unable to become the tribal chief, what are the obligations of that pastor?

1. The chief medicine man preaches at least thirty-five Sundays a year, and in most large churches the expectation is forty or more Sundays a year. This tribal expectation often is resented by other medicine men on the staff.

2. The chief medicine man visits the hospitals *at least* twice a week.

3. The chief medicine man buries the dead. It is essential that the chief medicine man officiate at the funeral services of the prominent members of the tribe. The responsibility for the funeral services for nonmembers can be delegated to an assistant medicine man.

4. The chief medicine man attends, although someone else may preside, all meetings of the tribal council.

5. The chief medicine man officiates at other important tribal ceremonies such as anniversaries, dedications, weddings, baptisms, and reception of new members and fulfills other priestly responsibilities.

6. The chief medicine man determines the nature and extent of his or her own involvement in intertribal (ecumenical and denominational) activities and events rather than allowing those decisions to be made by persons from other tribes. Most tribal members resent persons from other tribes placing expectations on their medicine man.

7. The chief medicine man calls on the prospective new members from that slice of the population that represents the tribe's number one priority in recruiting new members.

8. The chief medicine man, by action more than words, models the acceptable behavior patterns for other members of the tribe.

That is a relatively short list and some senior ministers believe this list is the only non-negotiable component of their role. That is not completely true. There remains the role of chief administrative officer.

What Does the Chief Administrative Officer Do?

In a few large congregations the role of tribal chief is filled by a layperson while the highest paid ordained minister on the staff functions as the number one medicine man and preaching minister. The third role, that of chief administrative officer, is filled by another staff person, usually an ordained minister. In effect, the three facets of the senior minister's role—tribal chief, number one medicine man, and chief administrative officer—are assigned to three different individuals.

This arrangement rarely arouses the widespread endorsement of the laity. Some are convinced it is unnecessarily redundant and excessively expensive. Others do not understand it. Most find it incompatible with their model of the role of the senior minister.

One of the reasons most laypersons prefer to see the senior minister accept and fill all three roles is that it simplifies life. Many questions and problems that arise in a large church are very complex. To whom do I take my concern or my question? The tribal chief? The number one medicine man? The chief administrative officer? Lay people naturally find life to be simpler if the same person fills all three roles. That means the senior minister's jurisdiction includes all of their concerns and questions.

In the vast majority of large churches the senior minister is expected to be and does function as the chief administrative officer of that congregation. That pattern obviously influences the content of this list of responsibilities of the chief administrative officer.

1. The chief administrative officer either (a) administers the organizational life of the large parish or (b) takes responsibility for seeing that this is done.

2. The chief administrative officer makes sure there is an adequate system for the care of members and monitors the system to make sure it is working. The actual operation of that system of congregational care usually is carried out largely by others.

3. The chief administrative officer accepts the primary responsibility for combatting the "cutback syndrome" that plagues nearly all large and long established congregations. The symptoms of this syndrome include suggestions such as "With attendance no more than it is, why don't we cut out that Thursday (or Saturday) evening service for people who cannot be here on Sundays?" or "Both of those adult classes are shrinking, why don't we merge them into one class?" or

"Why don't we have just one youth group for all high school kids? That would make it easier to get counselors."

One creative response to this syndrome is to insist on starting one new group, worship service, class, choir, or circle whenever any such subgroup or program is terminated so there is no reduction in the total scope and size of the ministry.

4. The chief administrative officer cooperates with the tribal chief in assuming that new members and new groups are assimilated and gain a sense of belonging to that tribe.

5. The chief administrative officer monitors the whole parish system to ensure that all the components of the total ministry and program are consistent with and reinforce the basic values, role, and goals of that congregation.

6. The chief administrative officer learns how to work effectively in a multiple staff setting. This is of crucial importance since the chief administrative officer is the key person in modeling staff behavior in a multiple staff arrangement.

7. The chief administrative officer defines a consistent model of staff relationships and consistently supports that model. The actual creation of the operational model may be a cooperative effort involving most or all members of the staff, but someone must accept the responsibility for holding the staff to that operational model.

8. The chief administrative officer conducts the staff meetings and models a style of staff behavior for staff meetings *or* accepts the responsibility for the operation of a system in which various staff members take turns presiding at staff meetings.

9. The chief administrative officer accepts the responsibility for clarifying both the role and the expectations of each program staff member.

10. The chief administrative officer accepts the responsibility that a response will be forthcoming to all complaints about the staff and complaints by staff.

11. The chief administrative officer (a) frequently expresses appreciation for the work of individual staff members, (b) attempts to provide built-in opportunities for staff members to gain a sense of

satisfaction from their work, (c) does not express nor encourage the expression of unattainable dreams for the model of staff relationships, and (d) does not pit one staff member against another. These four "rules" can drastically reduce complaints by staff.

12. The chief administrative officer affirms both the functional and the relationship dimensions of each staff member's work.

13. The chief administrative officer recognizes the distinction between delegation and abdication. It is essential that certain responsibilities in the large church be delegated to staff members and lay volunteers. That is not the same as abdicating responsibility.

14. The chief administrative officer displays a consistent and predictable leadership style.

Much has been written comparing a variety of leadership styles of senior ministers such as authoritarian or directive versus democratic or cooperative versus laissez faire or permissive.

While the results-oriented lay leadership tend to endorse a very directive leadership style by the senior minister, this writer's studies of large church staffs suggest there is not one "best" style. It is not difficult to find members of the professional staff and lay leaders who express great satisfaction with a senior minister who is very directive while nearly as many staff members and lay leaders can be found who express strong appreciation for the senior minister who follows a more democratic leadership style. Although less numerous, it is possible to find staff members and lay leaders who are supportive of a senior minister who follows a comparatively nondirective or permissive leadership style.

The only "bad" leadership style appears to be the leader who does not follow a predictable and consistent pattern. The leader who is perceived as shifting, without warning, from being very permissive to very directive to very democratic to some other undefinable style usually imparts an extremely demoralizing impact on staff members, lay leaders, and the entire organization. Most people can adapt, respond to, and survive any leadership style as long as it is predictable and consistent.

114

15. The chief administrative officer recognizes that the Second Law of Thermodynamics applies to large churches and to multiple staff arrangements.

This famous law of physics originally was articulated in 1824 explaining that when energy in one form is converted to another form, some of it is lost, regardless of the efficiency of the machine. Subsequently this theory has been expanded to the broader concept that everything runs down as entrophy increases. In recent years this concept has been applied to the study of social institutions, traffic jams, economic cycles, and political parties.

This theory of dissipative structures helps to explain why adding a second ordained minister to the staff of the growing church does not double the productive capability of the ministerial staff, why long-established large congregations require more staff than relatively new congregations of the same size, and why the worship attendance-to-membership ratio in the large church declines as the decades roll past.

If the chief administrative officer understands the Second Law of Thermodynamics, it can be helpful in diagnosing and responding creatively to evolutionary changes in the large church with a multiple staff.

16. The chief administrative officer is aware of the distinction between a "transactional" leadership style and a "transforming" leadership.[2] The former focuses on achieving goals that have been established earlier. The second requires the leader to shape, alter, influence, elevate, and direct the motives, values, and goals of the members of an organization. If the tribal chief follows a transforming approach to leadership, the chief administrative officer may need only to follow a transactional style and vice versa.

17. If the chief administrative officer is to be a transforming leader, it is necessary to go beyond the traditional requirements of skill and strategy, which are useful in implementing previously defined goals, and develop a theory of action for institutional change. To be able to act effectively on the insight gained from an application of the Second

Law of Thermodynamics, the senior minister needs a coherent and consistent theory of intervention.[3]

What Does This Mean?

The presentation of these three lists is not simply an attempt to devise a clever format for identifying the responsibilities of the senior pastor in a large church. There are other, more fundamental reasons for compiling these three lists.

First, and perhaps most important for some readers, a review of these lists reinforces a basic thesis of this book, serving as the senior pastor of a large congregation is not an easy assignment! It is a very difficult and extremely demanding responsibility and relatively few ministers have the necessary gifts, talents, and skills to fulfill such an assignment.

Second, this approach can help the reader identify three different sets of expectations that are placed on the senior minister in most large congregations.

Third, by defining these three facets of the role of the senior minister, using anthropological, rather than biblical or theological categories, it is possible to describe the perspective which many of the members of the congregation use as they develop a role-image of the senior pastor. There is an institutional, as well as an ecclesiastical and theological, frame of reference that can be used to define the role of a pastor. Some clergy, including many seminary professors, tend to use biblical and theological categories in defining the role of minister. Other ministers, including many denominational executives responsible for ministerial placement, tend to use ecclesiastical and functional categories. This writer is convinced that many lay persons think in anthropological terms as they define the role of the senior minister for their tribe.

Fourth, while the role of the senior minister in the large church can be defined using these three categories of tribal chief, number one medicine man, and chief administrative officer, it would be a serious error to interpret this as a recommendation that the three roles be filled by three different individuals.

Persons who conceptualize reality in functional terms may be tempted to use this chapter as the basis for a recommendation that the staff should include one person for each role. That is *not* the reason behind the definition of these three roles. This conceptual framework is used for analytical purposes, not as an outline for building a staff. The vast majority of laypersons think in relational terms and thus are much more comfortable when the senior minister in the very large congregation serves as the tribal chief, the number one medicine man, and also as the chief administrative officer!

Fifth, the application of these three categories may be useful for some senior ministers as they reflect on the behavior setting in which they find themselves, as they decide between what they will do themselves and what they will delegate to others and as they order the priorities on their time.

Sixth, this threefold definition of the role of the senior pastor can be useful on those rare occasions when (a) the associate minister is called to be the successor to the departing senior pastor or (b) the senior pastor and the associate minister trade positions and exchange roles and the associate minister becomes the new senior pastor.[4]

Finally, and most important of all for the successor, regardless of how a senior minister responds to the demands of these three roles, it is vitally important for the welfare of the successor that when the senior minister resigns, retires, or departs, all three roles be vacated!

How Do We Choose and Supervise Staff?

Two overlapping questions that come up repeatedly in conversations with senior ministers concern (a) the tenure of "inherited" staff who remain from the era of the previous senior minister and (b) the difficulties in constructive supervision of program staff.

One approach to the first question requires the intervention of a strong committee when the senior minister announces a departure date *or* before the process is completed for the selection of a successor. In operational terms this usually means that all other staff members are advised they may be expected to resign sometime in the future. In some cases every program staff member, including the secretary to the senior minister, is asked to submit a resignation dated six or eight months or a year after the arrival of the new senior minister.

This means the newly arrived senior minister, instead of being the villain who decides who must be dismissed, becomes the hero who decides which resignation will not be accepted.

While this procedure has much to commend it, it has two price tags. First, there is a risk that the most valuable staff members, who usually find it easy to secure a new position, are tempted to move during this period of uncertainty. The second disadvantage is that the procedure creates a long period of uncertainty which may immobilize program planning and development efforts.

A related approach is less rigorous, and perhaps equally effective. The lay leadership quietly informs all program staff members, including the secretary to the senior minister, that the new senior minister will be given the authority to build a new staff and that decisions on terminations and tenure will be made by the new senior minister. Thus the initiation of the idea that changes may be necessary is carried out by the lay leadership, not by the new senior minister. That is an important distinction!

Both approaches are based on the assumption that the senior minister is (a) the chief administrative officer of the parish and (b) responsible for the overall life, ministry, and program of the parish. If it is assumed that the new senior minister should not have the authority to build a program staff, his or her area of responsibility should be decreased accordingly.

Another approach to responding to inherited staff is to go back to the third chapter and suggest that the procedure for choosing and supervising staff should be consistent with the model chosen for staff relationships.

Obviously this discussion is largely irrelevant to those large churches that have a tradition of changing senior ministers every four or five years. Most of them cannot afford the loss of continuity in relationships and program that would be part of the cost of rebuilding a staff to complement a new senior minister. In most large congregations the senior pastor has the basic responsibility for supervising the program staff. In a few large congregations that responsibility rests with program and/or personnel committees. The suggestions offered here apply to both systems.

First, the procedure for planning and review sessions with program staff members should not be tied directly to decisions on (a) compensation and (b) tenure. Those two issues should be handled in different meetings in different physical settings.

Second, the emphasis or style should be one of "affirm and build" rather than "criticize and change."

Third, the one-to-one sessions with each program staff member should *always* begin with the staff member's agenda, not with the concerns, frustrations, or unfulfilled dreams of the senior minister!

Fourth, in most congregations the senior minister would be well advised to have quarterly meetings individually with each program staff member.

Mr. C. Philip Alexander, a management and organization development consultant in Ann Arbor, Michigan, has suggested a simple format for this process using three sheets of paper, each divided into two sections by a vertical line. On the first sheet the staff member responds to the question, "What is your job and what support do you expect of this church and of the senior minister?" On the left hand side of the sheet the staff member states his or her understanding of "my responsibilities to this congregation." On the right hand side the staff person explains "What I need from this congregation and from the senior minister in order to fulfill my responsibilities." This might include such things as more money for postage or secretarial help, the use of a particular meeting room, an hour every week with the senior minister, or additional resources for leadership development.

The second sheet of paper deals with achievements and needs for improvement. On the left-hand side the staff member lists his or her achievements during the past quarter. The senior minister may want to add to this list during their joint review. On the other half of the sheet the staff member lists the needs for improvement covering both personal and institutional deficiencies. The senior minister also may want to add to this list, but the primary emphasis during this review session should be on achievements.

On the third sheet of paper the program staff member lists on the left-hand side of that sheet the goals for which he or she has the staff responsibility for the coming quarter. (This list becomes the beginning point for next quarter's listing of achievements.) On the right-hand side of the sheet the staff member lists the action steps (specific program or task, beginning date, necessary resources, including people, target to be reached, timeline or schedule, and criteria for subsequent evaluation) necessary to achieve each goal.

If the senior minister will sit down with each staff member once a quarter and work through these three sheets of paper, the burden of supervision can be transformed into a very creative and productive shared experience. Among the many benefits of such a quarterly exercise are (a) the senior minister gains a clearer understanding of each staff member's work and accomplishments, (b) the personal and professional needs of the staff member are surfaced before they become counterproductive or disruptive frustrations, (c) internal communication is improved, (d) barriers to goal implementation can be identified in advance, (e) the staff member usually leaves each review session feeling affirmed, (f) a clearly defined beginning point is established for each review session, (g) both parties know what the rules are, (h) regular opportunities are created for redefining the responsibilities of each staff member, (i) two-way accountability is established between the senior minister and each individual staff member, (j) periodic opportunities are created for calling attention to deficiencies in performance, (k) each staff member receives individual attention from the senior minister at least four times a year, and (l) the senior minister becomes better informed about the total ministry and program of the parish.

This same system can be expanded to include similar sessions with a pastoral relations committee in which the senior minister prepares these same three sheets covering the senior minister's work.

How Do We Manage Our Time?

In the opening paragraph of this chapter, Howard Jones, a new senior minister, was raising questions about the management of time.

This is a complaint of thousands of ministers in churches of all sizes and types.

Without getting into an extended discussion of time management, three comments can be made.[5] The first is based on the major theme of this chapter. The more clearly the role of the senior minister is defined, the easier it will be to order priorities and allocate time.

The second comment is that every person has a choice of either managing one's own time and priorities or allowing the behavior setting to do it. This is the classic distinction between proactive and reactive. Do you allow the caller to determine how long you will be tied up by a telephone call, or do you determine the termination point for that telephone call? No one has absolute control over his or her time, but most of us may choose whether we spend 60 to 70 percent of our time reacting to the pressures placed on us or whether we spend 70 to 80 percent of our time in a proactive stance.

The third comment is derived from the format suggested earlier for the quarterly review of each program staff member's work. The senior minister who spends eight to twelve hours annually in these review sessions with each staff member usually will show a net gain of scores of hours by having a clearer understanding of what can be delegated, to whom it can be delegated, and the opportunities for such delegation— all of which are a part of the supervisory process. In other words, effective supervision of staff increases the opportunities for creative management of the senior minister's time.

When the discussion shifts from the role of the senior pastor to that of the associate minister, it is more than a change from one chapter to another. It also reflects a major change in congregational perspective and priorities. This point is illustrated by the fact that the basic outline for the history of most large congregations is organized around either (a) real estate, as the congregation moves from one meeting place to another during its history or (b) the pastorates of a series of senior ministers. It is rare to find a church history that is organized around the tenure of a series of associate ministers.

CHAPTER FIVE
The Associate Minister

"We certainly appreciate all you have done to welcome us here," exclaimed Jim Davis as he and his wife Laura finished their dessert at a fine restaurant with their hosts, John and Helen Stratton. The Strattons had driven out to the airport to pick up Jim Davis, the leading candidate to fill the vacant position of associate minister at First Church, and his wife who had been invited to come for this important interview. Helen Stratton was a member of the pulpit committee at First Church, and she had offered to meet Jim and Laura at the airport, take them to dinner, and bring them to the church for the 7:30 P.M. interview with the committee. John Stratton, a well-to-do businessman and an influential leader at First Church, was glad for this opportunity to meet the candidate and his wife.

As they talked over coffee, John felt the time had arrived that he could add his contribution to the evening's business. "We're delighted to have had this opportunity to get acquainted and we appreciate your company. While I'm not a member of the pulpit committee, let me tell you how things appear from the perspective of the ordinary member in the pew. We have an exceptional pastor in Henry Wilson, our senior minister, but he is badly overworked. Our last associate didn't do much to reduce the load on Dr. Wilson's shoulders, and I was not at all unhappy when he decided to move on to his own church. While I may be meddling in someone else's business, it seems to me the number one responsibility of the associate minister at First Church is to help and support the senior minister. If you can do that, we'll be happy with you and I'm sure you'll be happy here."

"Now John, that's not your business and you've got it all wrong," corrected Helen Stratton. "Our committee has talked this over with Dr. Wilson at length. We're looking for a young minister with some experience, such as Jim here, who will carry the basic staff responsibilities for Christian education, youth work, and community ministries. In addition to those specialized responsibilities, we expect the associate to function as a pastor in his own right, to preach about once a month, to conduct weddings and funerals, to visit, to call in the hospital, and to share in all phases of the professional ministry. Dr. Wilson has declared repeatedly that he is looking forward to a very productive team ministry in which he and the associate will share all aspects of the ministry. You make it sound like you're asking Jim if he is willing to be a flunky. We aren't looking for a flunky; we're looking for a second pastor!"

As he helped his wife on with her coat, Jim whispered into Laura's ear, "I sure like her definition of the associate's role here better than his!" Laura whispered back, "Always trust a woman's judgment!"

They arrived at First Church a few minutes after seven, and Mrs. Stratton introduced Jim and Laura to the early arrivals. As they were standing around getting acquainted, Mrs. Mary Becker, one of three women on the pulpit committee, steered Laura off to one corner. "Just between you and me, there's something your husband ought to know if he comes here," she said in a very low voice. "While all of us are happy with Dr. Wilson and we're all convinced he is the ideal minister for First Church, he has an ego as big as a house. If your husband decides to come here, he should realize that his number one job is to praise Dr. Wilson and to keep that big ego inflated. His number two job will be to protect Dr. Wilson from destructive criticism or any other negative comments. I know this won't come out during our meeting, but your husband better know that before he decides whether he wants to come to First Church. The basic role of the associate here is to praise and protect the senior minister. Our last associate wasn't willing to do that, and that's why this vacancy exists."

This incident, with minor variations on the basic theme, has been repeated in scores of large churches. Is the associate minister a full-fledged pastor in his or her own right who is expected to share, as a full pastor, in the pastoral ministry of that church? Or is the role of the associate minister to be a flunky, to serve as the alter ego, and one-person support group for the senior pastor, and to carry the staff responsibility for those functions which no one else wants or which no one else feels competent to carry?

Unfortunately, the answer to that extremely complex question is a very simple yes! In some large churches the associate is a full-fledged partner on the ministerial staff. In others the associate is an ordained flunky serving an apprenticeship. In many it is a shifting and unpredictable combination of the two.

This issue of an inadequately and inconsistently developed role is one reason behind a severe shortage in the ministerial marketplace—the very limited supply of clergy persons who feel a call to a vocation as a career associate minister. There is a tremendous need for persons to serve as associate ministers in large congregations with the expectation of remaining for one or two decades on the staff of the same church. To be more precise, there is a shortage of nonthreatening ministers with remarkably strong egos who are willing and able to do 99 percent of the getting along with the senior pastor, who have a gift for reinforcing the ego and role of the senior pastor, and who are married to a person who will not threaten the spouse of the senior minister. In addition, the candidates who would reduce this shortage should be willing to spend eight to fifteen years with the same congregation, be effective youth ministers, enjoy serving the elderly, possess unique gifts in leadership development, excel as teachers, not feel the desire to preach more than five to ten times a year, be able to relate to young adults, enjoy an ambiguously defined role, always wear a big smile, and be able to direct an effective new member recruitment program. One of the two ministers with all these gifts and talents recently accepted the call to become the senior pastor of a large church in Florida!

In addition to these two factors of ambiguity of role and excessive expectations, there are several other reasons why it is difficult to find effective staff members who feel a call to the position of associate minister as a vocation. A third is that nearly all seminaries train students to be pastors, not staff members. It is a simple fact of life that very few seminary graduates have the gifts, talents, experience, ego strength, training, and skills to be happy associate ministers. One result is that associate ministers are drawn in disproportionately large numbers from (a) women who are still finding it difficult to be placed as pastors, (b) ministers who must leave their present assignment and need a place, (c) seminary graduates who are not known to the persons responsible for recommending to congregations the names of potential associates, (d) ministers who are not sure of their call to the pastoral ministry and want an opportunity to test that call in a nonthreatening setting, (e) apprentices (f) ambitious and able young ministers with one or two pastorates behind them in small or middle-sized congregations who expect eventually to be the senior pastor of a large congregation and seek a couple of years of experience on the staff of a large church, (g) persons who feel a call to the ordained ministry, but do not like to preach, and (h) persons who want to specialize rather than serve as general practitioners, some of whom subsequently conclude they would rather be general practitioners.

A fourth factor behind the shortage of happy associate ministers in general, and the almost nonexistent examples of happy, long-term, and effective copastorates, is that in most large congregations the associate minister is a second class citizen.

Why Is the Associate a Second Class Citizen?

Perhaps the most influential single step that could be taken to improve the quality of staff performance and staff relationships in the typical large church would be to tackle the question of the status of the associate minister.

Before anything can be accomplished on a comprehensive basis for improving the second class role of the associate minister, however, it is necessary to identify the factors that have created this condition. While the following list is not presented as a definitive statement, it does illustrate several of the institutional factors behind this situation. In looking at this situation it is necessary to refer back to the deference pyramid that was mentioned in earlier chapters. In most institutions there is a "deference pyramid" which places subordinates in a lower position in the institutional "pecking order" and most people are expected to defer to those at the top of that pyramid.

1. The factor of age.

Our society has a built-in deference pyramid based on age. Younger persons are expected to "look up" to older people. (A simple illustration of this is that younger persons are expected to remember the names of older individuals, but older people are not expected to remember the names of younger people.) When the senior pastor is several years older than the associate minister, this tends to reinforce a secondary role for the associate.

A positive example of this is the senior pastor who wants to develop a collegial style with his associate and deliberately chooses an associate minister who is approximately the same age or older. This is a simple, but very important factor in building an effective team ministry!

2. The importance of seniority.

When the senior pastor has been serving a congregation for a longer period of time than the associate minister, this reinforces the secondary role of the associate. The greater the amount of seniority, the stronger the reinforcement of the deference pyramid with the associate in a lower position on the pyramid.

3. The impact of rank.

Churches, like seminaries, colleges, universities, and the military, place a major emphasis on titles and rank. The simplest illustration of this is the hierarchy of titles some churches have—senior pastor, associate minister, assistant minister, seminary intern, etc. The rank reflected in these job titles reinforces the deference pyramid with the senior pastor at the peak of the pyramid.

4. The influence of titles.

The typical situation has a senior pastor with a doctorate (either earned or honorary) and the associate minister with a master's degree or less. Thus the senior pastor often is referred to as "Doctor Jones" and the associate is called "Mr. Smith" or "Reverend Smith" or "Brother Sam" or simply "Sam," which reinforces the subordinate role of the associate.

The increasing number of young ministers with the Doctor of Ministry degree has created the very interesting situation where occasionally the senior pastor is "Mr. Jones" and the associate is "Dr. Smith." Some people feel uncomfortable with this because it runs counter to the deference pyramid.

5. The value of experience.

In varying degrees our society gives credit for experience in a vocation. Thus if the senior pastor has twenty-five years in the ministry and the associate minister is a recent seminary graduate, this contrast reinforces the secondary role of the associate.

6. The dominance of sexism.

Ours is still a male-dominated culture in North America and the male is perceived as superior to the female. While this tradition has begun to change, the dominant pattern is still one of placing the male at the top of the deference pyramid. The current pattern of a male senior pastor with a female associate minister reinforces the second class citizen role of the associate. (The impact of this factor will be far more visible in the 1980s when there will be an increase in the number of congregations with a female senior pastor and a male associate minister.)

7. The weight of tenure.

Many multiple staff congregations convey the expectation that the senior pastor will stay for a decade or longer, but that the associate will move on after two, three, or four years. This expectation also conveys the belief that the associate is less valuable, more expendable, and less important than the senior pastor.

8. The impact of peer group values.

The dominant value system of the clergy suggests that the associate minister is in a second class role. This is reflected by questions such as these: "Why did you decide to be an associate at your age?" "How long before you expect to get your own church?" "Aren't you getting tired of being an associate?" These questions reinforce the second-class status of the associate minister with the peer group.

9. The pressure of lay values and expectations.

A parallel can be seen in the value system and expectations of the laity: "I expect you'll be leaving us before long to have your own church." "We established the position of associate minister with the expectation that we could bring in a young minister fresh out of seminary and after a few years he would want to move on to have a church of his own." "It seems that whenever we get a good associate, some other church comes in and grabs him." "Honey, I don't think you ought to bother the pastor with such a trivial item," urged Mrs. Cole of her husband. "Why don't you wait until tomorrow and call the associate minister and see if she can help you?"

Each of these statements reflects a value system that suggests a good associate will be "promoted" to the role of pastor before long and thus move from a second class relationship to a first class role or that the associate minister can be "bothered" with questions too trivial to bring to the senior minister.

10. The influence of the ministerial placement system.

In both the appointment system and the call system denominations use a ministerial placement process which suggests that moving from the position of associate minister to becoming the pastor of a congregation is a "promotion." This pattern is more obvious in the denominations using an appointment system of ministerial placement than it is in the denominations using a call system, but it is present in the call system also. Many pulpit committees seeking a pastor, for example, will hesitate to extend a call to a pastor who has been serving a congregation for only two years, but that same committee will display little reluctance in extending a call to an associate minister who came to a post only fifteen months ago. They would hesitate to "steal" a pastor from a congregation which only recently called a minister, but they would feel much less restrained in opening the door to a "promotion" for an associate minister.

Another means of using the ministerial placement system for reinforcing the second class role of the associate minister is found in those denominations in which a seminary graduate often goes directly to become an assistant or associate minister. When the time comes to move, that minister often finds the only vacancies "open" to him or her are those which are open to anyone just out of seminary. After three, four, or five years as an associate the young minister "starts over" on the same salary level as the recent seminary graduate. There is no "credit" given for the experience as an associate minister.

11. The response to calling.

"When will the pastor be able to call on me?" Mrs. Harris asked her sister who had come to visit her in the hospital. "Didn't Reverend Sam stop in to see you a few minutes ago?" replied the sister. "He was coming out just as I was waiting for the elevator and he said you were feeling better." "Oh, yes, he was in here a little while ago," replied Mrs. Harris, "but he's just the associate. When's the pastor coming to see me?"

This is a widespread response to visitation by the associate minister and both illustrates and reinforces the second class role of the associate. (Incidentally, this is one problem that often is eliminated when the associate minister is as old or older than the senior minister.)

12. The role of the wife.

While this is not a universal pattern and is of less significance than it was in the 1950s, in many congregations the members establish a role and a set of expectations for the wife of the senior pastor. They often establish a different, and frequently less clear, role and a lesser set of expectations for the wife of the associate minister. This pattern of institutional behavior often reinforces the secondary role of the associate minister and is illustrated by what happened to the wife of one associate minister. He was the pastor of a 400-member congregation in a small town and then agreed to become the associate minister in a large city church. After they moved, she discovered she had left behind the role as a well-known and highly respected figure to become the anonymous wife of "Whatshisname."

13. The origins of the position.

Frequently a congregation creates the position of associate minister in order "to take part of the load off our overworked pastor." This is a substantially different motivation than creating a new position in order to staff a new ministry. Whenever a congregation adds a second minister to the staff "to carry part of the senior pastor's workload," the leaders usually end up creating an undefined role, with ambiguous responsibilities, few built-in satisfactions, and second class status on the deference pyramid.

14. The winners and losers syndrome.

In the typical congregation several responsibilities of the professional staff can be classified as "winners." These include preaching, hospital calling, home visitation, conducting weddings and funerals, teaching, and administration. These are the responsibilities that earn the appreciation and gratitude of the members. On the other side of the ledger are the "losers." These are the responsibilities that often receive considerable criticism and disapproval—sometimes for what is happening, frequently for what is not being done, and often for how those ministries and programs are being carried out. The list of "losers" includes the youth program, Christian education, evangelism, community ministries, social action, ecumenical affairs, and the ministry to single young adults.

A common method of reinforcing the second class role of the associate minister is to assign most or all of the "winners" to the senior pastor and ask the younger, and often relatively inexperienced, associate minister to be responsible for the "losers."

15. The leadership team.

Many congregations spend decades developing a leadership team consisting of one minister and a rotating group of lay leaders. (Frequently the longer the congregation has been in existence and the older the age of the members, the slower this process of rotating the lay leadership positions among the members.) After years of perfecting this model of a leadership team, such a congregation may create the position of associate minister and find someone to fill that newly created vacancy. However, rarely do they revise the model of a leadership team to include two ministers. The newly arrived associate minister often feels excluded, ignored, overlooked, bypassed, and neglected. The reason is that the old model of a leadership team causes the leaders to exclude, ignore, overlook, bypass, and neglect the recently arrived associate minister! The new associate feels like a second class citizen because the leadership model has not been revised to include a place for a second minister.

16. The impact of formal training.

With very rare exceptions theological seminaries train students to be pastors. They do not train students for a career as an associate minister. Thus the formal training is for one role, but the position calls for a different role. Whenever a person is asked to fill a role not consistent with earlier formal training and experience, this often tends to cause that individual to feel inadequate, uncertain, and uncomfortable. This discrepancy also confuses the expectations others hold of that person.

This may be seen in the sense of self-confidence and clear direction of the newly arrived professionally trained choir director whose clarity of expectation contrasts with that of the new associate minister.

17. The physical setting.

In many congregations it is easy to find the office of the senior pastor. It is just down the hall from the church office and just behind the secretary's office. It looks like a pastor's office and is large enough to accommodate three to ten visitors. Where is the associate's office? "Let's see, you go up those stairs, turn right at the top, go down the hall, walk across that big room and . . . maybe, it'll be easier if I show you. It's kind of hard to find and doesn't look like an office. It was a storage closet we remodeled when our new associate minister came."

18. The use of "ownership" language.

"I would like you to meet my new associate," declares the senior pastor. "She just arrived last week and I'm still in the process of breaking her into our routine here."

"John was my associate for six years back at the College Avenue church," observed the senior pastor, "and when I heard he was ready to move, I made a point of trying to get him right away. I surely am glad to have him here helping me."

These and similar comments reflect a common pattern in which the senior pastor suggests by the choice of words a sense of "ownership" of the associate minister. This language affirms and reinforces a second class role for the associate minister.

19. The lack of institutionalization.

"We had a seminary intern for several years, and then we decided to increase the stipend and have a full-time assistant minister. Our first one didn't work out very well, so we changed the job to director of Christian education and have had a woman in that position for three years. When she got married and left, we filled the position for nearly a year with a part-time retired minister who did only visitation. Then he moved to Florida, and we replaced him with a full-time youth minister. That didn't work out either, so we decided to redefine the job as a full-time generalist and we found a thirty-five-year-old minister with ten years experience who was getting a divorce and had to leave where he was. He served as our associate minister for two years and did a great job, but when he remarried, he left, and now we're in the market again. We know we need help, but we're not sure exactly what we're looking for."

The only response anyone can make with certainty to that speech is that congregation has not yet defined and institutionalized that position. Any minister who accepts it almost certainly will be met with conflicting expectations! It is still a vague and undefined "accessory" position, not a defined role.

20. The importance of satisfactions.

Every person is sustained and encouraged by a sense of satisfaction in what he or she is accomplishing. This is one reason that certain occupations and vocations are especially attractive, despite comparatively low financial rewards.

An outstanding example of this is the pastor who may be encountering many frustrations, but who is sustained by being able to fulfill "the call to preach." There are many other satisfactions and affirmations for the typical pastor. Some of these come as the pastor fulfills the responsibilities described as "winners" in item 14 above.

By contrast, however, the "losers" in that same list do not produce an equal quantity or quality of satisfactions. This means the "total compensation" of the associate is substantially less than that of the senior pastor, which reinforces the second class role of the associate.

The difference in the satisfactions available to the associate minister in contrast to the senior pastor is increased by the availability of support systems. Most senior pastors have a support system available to them through the session, board, council, vestry, pastoral relations committee, "the pastor's cabinet," or some similar group. Rarely is an equivalent support group available to the associate minister!

What does all of this mean? Why bother with this lengthy checklist? What is the purpose of this list?

There are three major reasons for looking at this list of factors which reinforce a second class role for the associate minister.

First, it will not be possible to upgrade the vocational role and the professional effectiveness of the associate minister until most of these barriers are eliminated. These barriers cannot and will not be removed until they are identified. In effect, this is a diagnostic list. Each congregation with an associate minister will have to write and implement its own prescription in response to this list. An outsider can perform the diagnosis, but the insiders will have to decide on their response to that diagnosis.

Second, there is an increase in the number of ministers who are seeking the opportunity to serve as copastors or in a team ministry. This pattern is supported by a number of lay persons in congregations that traditionally have been served by a senior minister and an associate minister.

One method of increasing the chances for an effective and lasting team ministry, or copastorate, is to remove most of the barriers that have relegated the associate minister to a second class role.

Finally, this list can serve as an agenda item for staff retreats in those large congregations where traditionally the agenda at staff meetings is dominated by "business" and functional concerns and limited attention is given to improving the quality of staff relationships.

What Does Our Associate Do?

One of the half dozen most common reasons for the comparatively short tenure of so many associates, for their lack of feeling needed and appreciated, for the widespread lay discontent with the productivity of associate ministers, and for the low level of morale among many holders of this office is primarily a product of the institutional setting. If one goes back to the list of "winners" and "losers" identified in item 14 in the previous section, it will be noted that one of the differences between the two lists is that most of the "winners" tend to have a high degree of visibility to the members, while most of the "losers" are low visibility functions of ministry. In other words, while the senior minister in most large churches functions within the context of a highly visible and clearly defined set of expectations and with the support of a highly structured institutional setting, many members do not know what the associate does because the associate minister has a more ambiguous role, a less structured setting, and responsibilities that tend not to be seen by most of the members. In most large congregations the reporting system makes the problem worse, rather than alleviating it.

This problem can be described from another perspective by contrasting the visibility of the work of the full-time "general practitioner" associate minister with the part-time single-function associate who carries only one clearly defined responsibility such as directing the choir, teaching, visitation, or youth work. The role of the typical general-practitioner associate minister often is filled with ambiguity and rarely is structured in terms of expectations, accountability, and evaluation. A common result is a frustrated associate minister, a disappointed congregation, a disillusioned senior minister, and an unproductively short pastorate.

A frequent symptom of this condition is the question, "What does our associate minister do?" That's a loser! A far better question is, "What is our associate minister doing to help us implement our congregational goals?" The most productive responses to that question include the six components that follow.

The first, obviously, is for a unified congregation to be functioning within the framework of a series of specific, attainable, measurable, visible, and widely supported goals. This is the single most effective means of producing a happy and effective staff team!

The second component is a clearly stated and highly visible line of accountability between the associate minister and the congregational leadership. A simple example of this would be for the associate minister to submit to the monthly Board meeting a one-page statement describing what he or she did during the past month. The best format for this monthly report is to use an outline consisting of the congregational goals that relate to the associate's responsibilities. Under each item, or goal, in this outline the associate minister describes in brief, precise, and clear language what he or she did to help implement that congregational goal. For example, under the goal "Care of Members" might be written, "I called in each of the three hospitals twice a week." Under the goal of "Personal and Spiritual Nurture" might be written, "Prepared for and taught four sessions of the Bethel Series." This monthly report helps give visibility to many of the low visibility responsibilities of the associate minister. It also requires the Board to be able to identify purposes, role, and goals.

A third component is to provide regular in-service training experiences to help clarify the role of the associate minister. Very few associate ministers have had first hand experiences with a large church. A useful response to that common fact of life is to ask the associate minister to spend two or three days working with an experienced associate minister in another large, similar church in another city of about the same size or somewhat larger.

The fourth part of this response is to make sure the associate minister has some "winners" as well as "losers" (see item 14 in the previous section of this chapter) in his or her portfolio.

The fifth element in this response is to institutionalize a system of accountability. One method is for the associate minister to take the initiative in creating the system of accountability. For example, once a week the associate minister places on the desk of the senior minister a list of what he or she expects to do during the following seven days.

Each week thereafter the associate minister submits a carbon copy of that list, having checked off what was accomplished, along with a list for the coming week of what he or she intends to do including items from the previous week that were not accomplished. This procedure also (a) provides a structured format for discussions between the senior minister and the associate on expectations, changes in responsibilities, work load, implementation of responsibilities, and shared responsibilities, (b) enables the senior minister to see the range and weight of the work load of the associate minister, (c) clarifies expectations for the associate minister, (d) provides some satisfaction for the associate minister in checking off that weekly list, (e) improves the quality of internal communication, and (f) reduces the chances of destructive tension, arising from what was not accomplished, but rarely is discussed openly and freely.

Another method, which places the initiating responsibility on the senior minister, rather than on the associate minister, was described on pages 119-120.

The final element in this six-part response is to encourage the associate minister to concentrate his or her time and energy, insofar as is possible, in those responsibilities which best utilize the gifts, talents, and skills of the associate minister. In other words, insofar as is possible, ask the associate minister to specialize in what he or she does best.

What Are the Safe Assumptions?

The world is filled with two sets of assumptions. One set is based on the belief that man is innately good and that if good people work together with good intentions, it is possible to produce a society with zero defects. The second set of assumptions is based on a combination of the doctrine of original sin, Murphy's law, and the probability that when the freshly-prepared mid-afternoon snack is dropped, it will land jelly-side down. The first set can be described as fail-disaster assumptions. If things do not go as anticipated, the result is a disaster. The second is known as a fail-safe approach. It assumes that something will malfunction—although the potential malfunction may not always be identified in advance—so a backup system is installed. If there is no malfunction, everything is safe. If there is a malfunction, the backup system prevents disaster.

Associate ministers must choose between these two sets of assumptions. It is suggested that associate ministers consider five fail-safe assumptions.

1. The newly arrived associate minister must define his or her role or be sure it is adequately defined. The fail-disaster assumption is to assume that someone else, such as the predecessor, the senior minister, the Board, or a personnel committee, will define a role that the new associate minister will feel comfortable in, that will not be filled with ambiguity, and that will produce meaningful satisfactions.[1]

2. The associate minister will have to do at least 85 percent, and perhaps 99.9 percent of the getting along with the senior minister. That may be an unfair load to place on the associate minister, but it is a fail-safe assumption.

3. The associate minister must accept 100 percent of the responsibility to build in a system of accountability and to provide adequate visibility for his or her work.

4. The associate minister who wants to "do my own thing" should see the traditional hierarchical ecclesiastical structure originated by Cyprian as an asset, not a liability. By contrast, the concept of a team ministry or a copastorate makes far heavier demands on the second minister on the staff for self-discipline and for subordinating his or her interests to a lower priority.

This point was stated very clearly by Peter Drucker when he wrote,

There is much talk these days about the individual's "doing his thing." But the only organization structure in which this is remotely possible is a hierarchial one. It makes the *least* demands on the individual to subordinate himself to the goals of the organization or to gear his activities into the needs and demands of others. Altogether, the more clearly a structure defines work, authority, and relationships, the fewer demands does it make on the individual for self-discipline and self-subordination.[2]

137

5. The associate minister must decide in advance, and be prepared to act on his or her response to the question, "Is my primary loyalty to the senior minister or to this congregation?" The safe assumption is that if the associate minister struggles with this question before it becomes an issue, it will be easier to develop a response that is consistent with the values and goals of the associate minister, than if the issue is ignored until a divisive question arises, and the associate minister is forced to make a choice on primary loyalties.

What About Productivity and Compensation?

Among the more troublesome issues that repeatedly arise in relation to the associate minister are the overlapping questions about productivity and compensation. Four generalizations may shed some light on these questions.

First, always compare the quality and quantity of the associate minister's work and productivity with that of other associate ministers, not with that of the senior minister. This will be more work for those making the comparisons, but will be far more helpful. It is reasonable to compare the work and productivity of two ministers in a copastorate in which they share equally all responsibilities and receive exactly the same compensation. It is completely unfair, however, to compare the work of a comparatively inexperienced younger associate minister in a relatively ambiguous role with that of the more experienced senior minister who has a much more structured setting.

Second, before beginning to make any judgments on the productivity of the associate minister, the congregational leaders should distinguish between the "apprenticeship" associate minister, who comes to the staff directly from seminary, and the "career associate," who may have ten, twenty, or thirty years of experience. Obviously, it is reasonable to expect the productivity of the second to be far higher than the productivity of the first.

Third, in a church with two full-time ordained ministers, the total compensation "package" (salary, housing, utilities, pension, educational allowance, health insurance, etc.) of the less experienced and

138

younger associate minister usually is equal to 50 to 70 percent of the total compensation of the senior minister.

Fourth, the total compensation of the mature and experienced career associate minister usually is equal to approximately 70 to 85 percent of the senior minister's total compensation. (This last generalization does NOT apply to the mature associate minister who is anticipating retirement in a few years and who specializes in visitation!)

Far more important than financial compensation, however, is the satisfaction the associate minister derives from being part of the staff in a large congregation that joyfully accepts the challenge of its unique role as a big church, that has carefully developed the staff team appropriate to that role, and that has recognized the importance of good staff relations.

Notes

Chapter One: The Large Church

1. For a more detailed analysis of how churches respond to lay volunteers see Lyle E. Schaller, *Survival Tactics in the Parish* (Nashville: Abingdon, 1977), pp. 80–90 and Douglas W. Johnson, *The Care and Feeding of Volunteers* (Nashville: Abingdon, 1978).

2. An extended discussion of the differences between large groups and small groups is found in Lyle E. Schaller, *Effective Church Planning* (Nashville: Abingdon, 1979), pp. 17–63.

3. For a discussion of the debate over efficiency and economy versus redundancy see Lyle E. Schaller, *Parish Planning* (Nashville: Abingdon, 1971), pp. 221-40.

4. For a different set of categories in looking at churches by type see Lyle E. Schaller, *Hey, That's Our Church!* (Nashville: Abingdon, 1975).

5. An excellent description of the distinctive characteristics and unique assets of the small church can be found in Carl Dudley, *Making the Small Church Effective* (Nashville: Abingdon, 1978) and Douglas Alan Walrath, *Leading Churches Through Change* (Nashville: Abingdon, 1979), pp. 14-20 and 64-89.

6. For a brief critical review of the Carl Rogers approach to leadership and why it may be inappropriate for a senior pastor see Christopher Lasch, "Books Considered," *The New Republic* (March 31, 1979), 30–31.

7. A technical definition of the "behavior setting" and its importance can be found in Roger G. Barker, *Ecological Psychology* (Stanford University Press, 1968), pp. 18–34 and 137–85.

8. An elaboration on this contrast between the small church and the large church can be found in William H. Willimon and Robert L. Wilson,

Preaching and Worship in the Small Church (Nashville: Abingdon, 1980), chapters 3 and 4. For a more detailed discussion of the negative impact of the landlord role see Lyle E. Schaller and Charles A. Tidwell, *Creative Church Administration* (Nashville: Abingdon, 1975), pp. 183–91.

Chapter Two: Staffing the Large Church

1. For a more extended discussion of these first seven factors see Lyle E. Schaller, *Understanding Tomorrow* (Nashville: Abingdon, 1976).

Chapter Three: Models of Staff Relationships

1. In a sample of 88 churches, one researcher found that 61.2 percent of all senior ministers rated staff relationships as "basically good," while 75 percent of the assistant ministers rated their relationship(s) with the other minister(s) on the staff as "basically poor." On a scale of 1 to 5 with the best possible staff relationships graded as 5 and the worst possible as 1, 95 of the 136 assistants gave a grade of 1 or 2 to staff relationships in their churches, while 42 of the 80 senior pastors gave a grade of 4 or 5 to staff relationships. Kenneth R. Mitchell, *Psychological and Theological Relationships in the Multiple Staff Ministry* (Philadelphia: The Westminster Press, 1966), pp. 261-62.

2. For an excellent brief introduction to a doctrine of multiple staff ministry see Marvin T. Judy, *The Multiple Staff Ministry* (Nashville: Abingdon, 1969), pp. 17–39. For a useful kit to help members of a multiple staff team reflect on their relationships, investigate *Building the Multiple Staff* prepared by and available through the Centre for Christian Studies, 77 Charles Street West, Toronto, Ontario M5S 1K5.

3. Robert C. Worley, *Dry Bones Breathe* (Chicago: Center for the Study of Church Organizational Behavior, 1978).

4. For a popular introduction to the subject see Lucille Forer, *The Birth Order Factor* (New York: Pocket Books, 1976) or James T. Baker, "First-Born Sons and Brothers' Keepers," *The Christian Century* (November 22, 1978), 1133–35. For a more detailed research report see Walter Toman, *Family Constellation,* 3d ed. (New York: Springer Publishing Company, 1976).

5. Lest anyone take these paragraphs too literally, it should be noted that parents can and do alter family constellation patterns. For example, some large families include two or three children who as adults display the characteristics of a typical first-born. Likewise, the time interval between births often influences developmental patterns.

6. Married readers who do not understand the term "getting along" are advised to turn to their spouse who will have no difficulty explaining the concept.

Chapter Four: The Senior Minister

1. John Kenneth Galbraith, *The Nature of Mass Poverty* (Boston: Houghton Mifflin Company, 1979).

2. For a detailed explanation of this analysis of leadership styles see James MacGregor Burns, *Leadership* (New York: Harper & Row, 1978).

3. For an excellent introduction to the theory of intervention and the theory of action see Chris Argyris and Donald H. Schon, *Increasing Professional Effectiveness* (San Francisco: Jossey-Bass Publishers, 1975).

4. It appears that the congregational polity churches that do not have a high-church theology of the office of minister and are not highly liturgical offer a more supportive context for an exchange of roles by the senior pastor and the associate minister than do other churches. For one account of a successful exchange of roles see W. Robert DeFoor, "But Baptists Don't Do It That Way!" *The Baptist Program* (January 1978).

5. A more comprehensive discussion of this subject is found in Speed B. Leas, *Time Management* (Nashville: Abingdon, 1978).

Chapter Five: The Associate Minister

1. For a suggestion on one response to this issue see Lyle E. Schaller, *Survival Tactics in the Parish* (Nashville: Abingdon, 1977), pp. 166–78.

2. Peter Drucker, *Management* (New York: Harper & Row, 1974), p. 526.

254
Sch2m